EXAMINING

The Media

The Media

Barbara Connell · Jude Brigley · Mike Edwards

Hodder & Stoughton

A MEMBER OF THE HODDER HEADLINE GROUP

British Library Cataloguing in Publication Data

Connell, Barbara H.
  Examining the media
  1. Mass media 2. Mass media – Problems, exercises, etc.
  3. Communication 4. Communication – Problems, exercises, etc.
  I. Title II. Brigley, Jude III. Edwards, Mike
  302.2'3

ISBN 0 340 65853 3

First published 1996
Impression number   10 9 8 7 6 5 4 3 2 1
Year   1999 1998 1997 1996

Typeset by Wearset, Boldon, Tyne and Wear.
Printed in Great Britain for Hodder & Stoughton Educational, a division of Hodder Headline Plc, 338 Euston Road, London NW1 3BH by The Bath Press, Bath

Contents

Acknowledgements

We would like to thank a whole range of people who have helped us to prepare this book. We have been fortunate in having the support of Media Education Wales and owe a particular debt of gratitude to its workers, Cathy Grove, Tom Barrance and Terry Morgan. The Welsh Joint Education Committee (WJEC) in Cardiff has also been very supportive in developments in GCSE Media Studies and willingly made material available which is not normally accessible. Roberta Harris has been unfailingly helpful over the years.

So many teachers and students have influenced this book that it would be impossible to name them all individually. We are grateful for their forbearance and hope that we have reflected some of their enthusiasms and expertise. To the teachers who have put up with our enthusiasms, engaged us in dialogue about what we do and why we do it, and from whom we have unconsciously or otherwise borrowed, our thanks.

Many of the examples in this book come from media students who demonstrate that this is a subject that combines in exciting ways the academic and vocational aspects of the curriculum. In particular, we would like to thank Mollie Baxter from Lancaster, Damien Doyle from Northern Ireland, Chloe Tilley from Nottingham and Trevor Williams from Wales for the use of their work. We hope that we have represented your work well. Our thanks too to all the media students who appear in this book. No doubt by the time this book is published they will have gone on to achieve great things; they may even be working in the very important industries which are at the heart of this book and with which we are all involved.

Introduction

We are all involved in the media and we all have views on aspects of the media. We talk about films, programmes, records, pop stars and magazines we have seen, heard and read. We have views on what we like and what is good. In many ways our lives are organised by the media; we shape our days around media events. We watch breakfast television, listen to the radio, play records, go to the cinema, watch a major sporting event, find time to read our favourite magazines and comics. So one of the most important reasons for studying the media is to explore the issues involved in our uses of the media.

All the activities in this book try to make you ask questions about the media and about your involvement with different kinds of media. The book also encourages you to link your involvement with the media to your own experiences of making media products during your media studies course. Even when you are doing media production work, you will be encouraged to pose questions about the ways in which you are undertaking the work. The final section of each chapter introduces some of the media theories and concepts you will need in order to carry out a deeper study of the media.

Getting going

1 How many different media can your group list? Now look through the contents list for this book again.
2 How many of the media can you identify from your list?
3 How many of your list were not present?
4 Did you have any surprises?
5 Were you disappointed in any way?

The answers to these questions will help you to begin thinking about the concerns and issues involved in a study of the media. You will also be using your own experiences with the various media – your media history. As the authors of this book, we suggest that you spend some time on a personal history of your involvement with the media. No generation has a bigger media history

© MEW

FIG 1.1 *Finding out what you need to know – in the classroom*

© MEW

FIG 1.2 *Finding out what you need to know – the press conference*

than your generation, because no previous generation has had access to so many different kinds of media and such a range of media products.

Start your study of the media by comparing your teenage involvement with the media with that of other older individuals (your parents, teachers, grandparents) at the same age. Choose someone in the 40–60 age range to interview and with whom you feel comfortable.

ACTIVITY

PERSONAL INTERVIEW QUESTIONS

The aim of these stimulus questions is to find out what experience of the main media the older people you interview had when they were teenagers. Do not feel that you have to use all of them. They are intended as conversation starters, so encourage the person you interview to be relaxed and to talk as much as he or she wants to. You should tape record your interviews if you can, and if your interviewee approves.

Radio
- When you were a teenager, did you listen to the radio?
- What was your favourite programme?
- Can you remember when it was on?

Television
- Do you remember your first experience of television?
- What memories do you have of early television?
- Did your parents allow you to watch what you wanted?

Film

- Did you go to the pictures as a teenager?
- Did you have a favourite star?
- What films did you like best?

Newspapers

- Did you read any newspapers as a teenager?
- Did your family regularly have newspapers delivered?

Magazines

- Did you have a favourite magazine?
- Where did you get your magazines from?

Comics

- Did you read comics as a child?
- Were you allowed to read comics as a teenager?

Popular music

- When did you buy your first record? What was it? What did you play it on?
- Did you have a favourite group/song/album?

When you have completed your interview, think carefully about whether the material you have gathered is different from your experience of the media. Prepare a short report (written or oral) for the rest of the class on what you have found out.

The important thing about this activity is that you become aware of the kinds of knowledge, skills and experience you already have of the media. These can be used as a starting point for further study. This does not mean that you will just be asked to do the things you are interested in already, but that the book will provide you with some new approaches to things you have perhaps not yet really thought about or been involved in. Examining the media means developing a whole range of practical, social and intellectual skills.

One attitude that all of us who are interested in the study of the media have to face is why we are interested in studying things which some people say are not serious, but really rather trivial. We hope that this book will not only help you to pass your examinations well, but will also give you good answers to those kinds of criticisms.

One of the reasons we have written this book is because we enjoy the media. This does not mean that we think everything in the media is good. After all, even fans of particular programmes or pop stars think that some bits are better than others. Good, bad, boring or mind-boggling, we think that by studying the media you are really forced to examine yourself and the world in which you live. This book raises questions about how we see ourselves and our relationships with others not only by asking you to consider media products like films and television programmes, but also by actively encouraging you to work on making media products. In our view, only when you combine doing with thinking and investigating do you really begin to examine the media.

How this book is organised

This book is divided into three parts:

- Part 1   The media concepts of forms, representations, organisations and audiences.
- Part 2   The main media forms defined by the GCSE syllabuses in England and Wales.
- Part 3   Examinations: the examples are mostly drawn from work done on the WJEC syllabus in Media Studies.

Some of you may prefer to concentrate on Parts 2 and 3 if you already have some experience of examining the media.

Each chapter is subdivided into three units which explore the concepts, forms and genres from different viewpoints. You should use the contents list to help you focus on media issues, practices and products which particularly interest you.

1

MEDIA CONCEPTS

1

Media forms and conventions

Looking at the world

We are all familiar with the phrase 'every picture tells a story', but what, exactly, does it mean?

ACTIVITY

Look at the montage in Figure 1.3 on page 4. You will see that it contains an assortment of pictures of people.
- Do they tell individual stories?
- Can you build up a story about the people and their lives from their representations?

Select three of the pictures and write a short profile about the people in them.
- Where are they from?
- What do they do?
- What are their names?
- How old are they?
- What are they like?

Discuss your ideas with the rest of your group.

Making stories

Do you think that the montage tells a collective story? Perhaps it would make more sense with additional captions which would help to anchor the meaning of the pictures as a whole. What do you think of the following captions?

- families
- summer dreamers
- memories.

Could you use them to incorporate all of the pictures in the montage?

ACTIVITY

Make a montage of photographs of people. You could collect photographs from home or select some from magazines. Mount your montage on sugar paper and ask other groups to add captions.

What you have been doing is constructing stereotypes: generalising about people because of the way in which they are presented to you. This is something that the media do all the time. Generalisations are used to represent something or someone specific and we, as media audiences, have become very adept at deconstructing the images and extracting a meaning – usually the meaning that the authors of the text want us to extract.

Pictures are constructed: someone takes them and the image is fitted into a frame.

FIG 1.3

Look back at the three photographs you selected from Figure 1.3:

- Who do you think took the photos? Why?
- Where was the photographer positioned?
- Are they posed photographs or simply snapshots?
- Have the photographs been cropped?

It is possible to alter the way someone reads a picture (or the story that we give to the picture) simply by altering the angle from which it has been taken, cropping it or adding a caption to it.

Obviously some pictures are more constructed than others. Look at the photograph in Figure 1.4. Clearly the man in it knows that a photograph is going to be taken and has carefully positioned himself to present a particular message.

© *Terry Morgan*

FIG 1.4

- What can you tell about the man from the photograph?
- Who could be the audience for this photograph?

If we are allowed to present ourselves in a photograph, we can present the image that we want other people to see. If someone else composes a photograph of us, it may not be the one that represents us in a way that we would like.

ACTIVITY

In pairs, write a list of ten words or phrases that you think best describe your partner, e.g. likes basketball; swims; drinks cola. Do not let your partner see what you write.

- Make a sketch for a photo of your partner showing these things.
- Do the same for yourself. How would you like to be represented?
- What image of yourself would you like to portray?
- Compare your ideas. How accurate were you both?

Usually the photographs that we see in newspapers and magazines (and even the ones we take when we are on holiday) represent the idea of the people (or the event) that the photographer wants to show.

More often than not, pictures do tell stories, but they tell the story from one particular point of view – one that usually comes from the person who is taking the picture or the institution that commissioned the picture, and not from the person whose picture is being taken.

ACTIVITY

As an individual, collect a selection of pictures from newspapers and magazines. See how you can alter their meanings by:

- cropping them
- extending them by drawing in what you think may be outside the frame

- juxtaposing them
- altering their captions
- adding speech bubbles
- adding extra items
- making things and/or people further apart (or closer).

Here you are in control and can present the meaning that you want; it is almost as if you were an editor, working with the photographer to present a meaning, through the image, to an audience.

ACTIVITY

MAKING A MONTAGE

Working in a small group, construct a montage of photographs which represent all the members of the group. Some of the photographs may show you, your family and friends; others may be representative of your interests and concerns. Use a range of images from a variety of sources: photo albums, magazines, adverts and pictures you have taken yourselves. Plan carefully and then display with care, using text where you think it is appropriate.

More things to do with the still image

1 Collect a series of pictures on a selected theme, such as heroes, families, romantics or teenagers, and make a large montage for classroom display.

2 Select three newspaper photographs which feature people. Add speech bubbles to alter the meaning.

3 With a partner, select several current newspaper photographs; carefully remove the captions from them then pass everything on to another pair. See if they can match the correct captions to the correct photographs.

4 If you have access to a camera, work in a small group to plan, take and display a photo-story entitled: Late for Class!

5 Collect a series of still images from any print sources and link them using text in order to create a narrative. If you have access to a video camera you could film each picture and add the text as a voice-over.

6 Look at Figures 1.5 and 1.6, two montages of photographs made by students in South Wales. Make your own montage to represent where you live.

What you have learnt

❶ *The meanings of single photographs can be changed depending on how they are interpreted by the audience.*

❷ *The meaning is often constructed by the photographer, but editing of the image can change the meaning.*

❸ *There are a variety of editing techniques which anchor the meaning of the photograph: captioning, cropping.*

❹ *Photographs can be linked in different ways to create new meanings: montage, juxtaposition, narrative.*

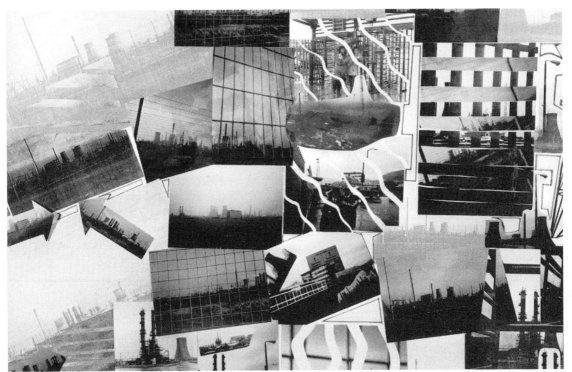

FIG 1.5

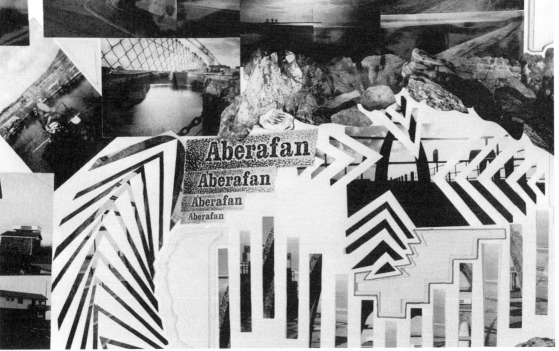

FIG 1.6

Listening in on the world

It seems strange that when television first appeared, many people thought radio was dead. Nobody would want to just listen when they could see and hear. In the 1990s radio is still a part of the daily life of millions of people all over the world. How much is it a part of your life?

ACTIVITY

PERSONAL SURVEY

❶ Where do you listen to the radio?
  (a) in your bedroom
  (b) in the car
  (c) waiting for the bus
  (d) with friends down the park
  (e) on the beach on holiday
  (f) in school
❷ What do you listen to?
  (a) music
  (b) weather forecasts
  (c) *The Archers*
  (d) the chart show
  (e) local news
  (f) national news

What are the most popular answers in your group? Why do you think this is?

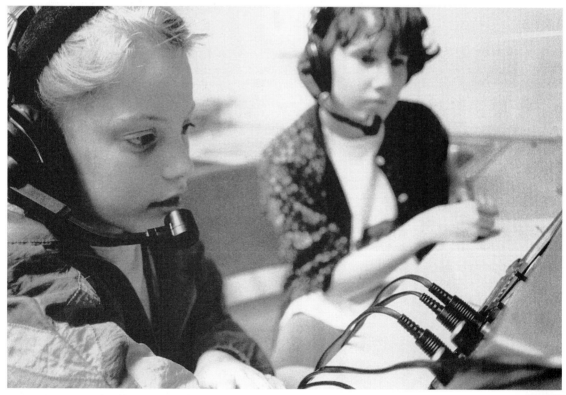

© *MEW*

FIG 1.7 *Radio presenting – starting young*

The radio audience

You are almost certainly one of the 40,804,000 people who in 1994 listened every week to a staggering 847,735,000 hours of radio broadcasting in Great Britain. We know this because in 1992 the Radio Joint Audience Research body (RAJAR) was set up to research the radio audience and it is telling us that radio is alive and well, even though there has been a slight decrease in the overall audience since television began in Great Britain.

So who are all these people, what do they listen to and, most importantly, why do they listen?

To start to answer questions like these, you need to learn how to research and present your findings to other people. The best place to start is with your own opinions, as these represent the way in which you think about the world.

Do you agree or disagree with the following statements?

- Teenagers prefer television to radio.
- Teenagers only listen to pop music on the radio.
- Teenagers are not interested in 'talk' radio.
- Teenagers don't listen to local radio.

Does everyone in your group agree on the answers?

It is most likely that they do. So should we leave it there? Well, you could. Your group is fairly representative of young people. However, as a media studies student you have to learn to question such views to see if they are true for young people generally.

Now try these questions:

1 Does it make a difference if your group comes from a city, town or village?
2 Does it make a difference whether your group is made up completely of boys or girls or is mixed?
3 Does it make a difference what languages you speak at home and in school?

We all feel that our opinions are common sense, but research may, sometimes, lead us to question the truth of our initial views and show us that common sense is not always enough. An important skill in this subject is questioning what we normally take for granted.

ACTIVITY

In this activity you are going to try and find out more about what the members of your group listen to on the radio. You are going to use an important media research technique, the **survey**.

Brief

In this survey you ask questions in order to find out:

(a) how much the selected group use radio, which programmes on which stations they listen to, and where they listen to them
(b) their attitudes to radio: their favourite stations, DJs, programmes, and reasons for listening.

You can either record responses using a tape recorder or ask classmates to fill in a questionnaire.

Method

You might find it useful to split the class, with some groups doing **(a)** and some doing **(b)**. The reason is that the questions you will be asking need different kinds of answers. The kinds of answers might lead you to use either a questionnaire or an extended interview as the best approach.

The first important thing is to construct the questions you want to ask. The first area **(a)** asks you to investigate using questions which need factual information. Questions which start with How much? How often? When? Where? are appropriate.

Why is a questionnaire the best way of conducting this survey?

The second area **(b)** asks you to investigate using questions which will help make clear the opinions of the respondents. Questions like 'Why do you like listening to the radio?', 'What do you like about your favourite radio presenter?' would be appropriate.

Why would recorded interviews be the best way of conducting this survey?

Before you ask the questions, test them to see if they give the right kind of information. Think about:
- the order of questions
- their usefulness for what you want to know
- the number of questions
- the ability of the respondent to answer
- the language of the questions.

Be on the look out for those questions which, when you try them out, do not really get the response you want. You now have a survey instrument: a questionnaire or interview schedule.

Sample

We suggest that about eight people for each group will be enough for the purposes of this research. If appropriate, the sample could be drawn from people outside your class to widen the research. Do make sure that the people are all the same age but that the groups are different in their composition: some groups should be all female; some groups all male; some groups mixed.

Presentation

The next task is to work out a variety of ways in which you could present the results of the research to the rest of the class. Do you want to report in written or oral form? Or do you want to be more ambitious and present in a media form like a radio interview or magazine article? Which would be the most effective method of presentation?

Conclusions

Finally, we would ask you to think about the range of conclusions reached by the different groups. Our guess is that there will not be a great deal of difference between them. You will probably find that the results confirm the answers to the personal survey you carried out at

the beginning of this unit. One obvious explanation for this would be that the sample is drawn from people who are likely to have the same kinds of interests. A less obvious explanation might be that some of the people who answered questions did not reveal everything, choosing to hide their real behaviour. These people want to give you the answer you expect.
- Are there any other disadvantages to survey methods?
- What would you say are the main uses and advantages of surveys?

Targeting the audience

All media organisations use survey techniques to research what their consumers want.

The BBC radio needs to persuade people to tune in to its programmes to justify its licence fee. Independent radio needs to finance itself through the number of advertisers who can be persuaded to advertise their products on the station: the bigger the audience, the more advertisements, the bigger the profit for the shareholders. All radio stations seek to increase their share of the available audience.

The BBC and independent radio are in direct competition for the listeners' attention.

ACTIVITY

Here are a few questions to test your general knowledge of the structure of national broadcasting in Great Britain and some radio conventions. A *Radio Times* or *TV Times* or the listings page of your local newspaper will help you if you are stuck.

❶ How are each of the following stations funded: through licence fee (BBC only) or advertising (all the others)?

    (a) Classic FM   **(b)** Radio 5
    (c) The World Service

(d) Atlantic 252   **(e)** Radio 1
(f) Talk Radio UK

2 Which independent national radio stations are being described?

(a) A populist alternative to Radio 3 with a service of light classical music.

(b) Its programmes concentrate on album rock music for the 20–45 year old market.

(c) It has to have at least 51 per cent speech-based programmes.

(d) It does not have a licence and broadcasts from Dublin.

When you discuss the answers, it should be clear that all radio organisations target their audiences. By this we mean that they try to create an image to attract a specific kind of listener group.

Image

All radio stations seek to establish their own distinctive image. This image is made up of a number of elements:

- the type of music played
- the attitude and accent of the presenters
- the relationship between speech and music
- the relationship between information and entertainment
- the relationship between local, regional and national issues
- the choice of types of programmes, e.g. bulletins, chat, quiz, plays, magazine, music
- the programme mix and the scheduling of programmes, as the audience changes during the day/night/week
- jingles, signature and theme tunes, live performances, self-advertising
- visual identity: logo, literature, advertisements on billboards, in cinemas, newspapers.

Use these categories to analyse a radio organisation of your own choice.

Market research

Through these kinds of strategies, radio stations seek to produce their own distinctive profile and package it for the target group. This profile is based on extensive market research to target clearly specific groups within any age range. The research will be based on groups who can be identified by such things as:

- locality
- musical taste
- nationality
- ethnic group
- class
- educational background
- self image.

Why do you think young people are an important target group for the media? Could radio do more to target young people?

ACTIVITY

MAKING RADIO PROGRAMMES

1 Choose five records which would appeal to 14–16 year olds in your school. They are to be played on a school's radio programme which is broadcast in the lunch hour. They will form part of a half-hour broadcast of news, views, chat and music. Write and present the introductions to the records. These should be brief and appropriate to the audience.

2 Who is your favourite radio presenter? Make a profile of the presenter. Think about such things as voice, relationship with audience, catchphrases, choice of music, guests, stories, etc. Plan a programme in the style of your presenter.

What do you know about radio?

Use these questions to develop your knowledge of the conventions of radio.

1 Which type of radio programme is most likely to feature a studio guest?
   (a) a news bulletin
   (b) a weather forecast
   (c) a radio commercial
   (d) a chat show

2 Which of these can be described as dialogue?
   (a) two singers singing together
   (b) two characters in a radio play conversing
   (c) two people reporting on a football match
   (d) a reporter quoting what someone else has said

3 Is the commentator:
   (a) the person in the studio reading the news?
   (b) the person who interviews the players?
   (c) the person who presents a sports show?
   (d) the person at the match telling you what happens?

4 Which of these can be described as a continuity device?
   (a) a trailer
   (b) an emergency news bulletin
   (c) a weather report
   (d) an outside broadcast

5 Which of these is a location recording?
   (a) a live concert
   (b) a studio-based play
   (c) an interview with a studio guest
   (d) a pre-recorded traffic bulletin

6 Which of these radio programmes has an 'open' narrative form?
   (a) a match commentary
   (b) a quiz programme
   (c) a soap opera
   (d) a news item

7 Which of these encourages an interactive approach from the listener?
   (a) a promotional competition
   (b) a studio interview with a pop star
   (c) a commentary on a football match
   (d) a weather report

8 Which of these is the most important quality for a newsreader on Radio 4?
   (a) a lively delivery in a local accent
   (b) the ability to pose challenging questions to politicians
   (c) precise intonation and clear, crisp delivery
   (d) to be well informed

9 Which is the best way to show a character's response to a situation on the radio?
   (a) a sound effect
   (b) a voice-over
   (c) a description
   (d) a soliloquy

10 Which of these types of radio programmes will be broadcast live?
   (a) a soap opera like *The Archers*
   (b) a quiz show like *Brain of Britain*
   (c) a radio play like *Under Milkwood*
   (d) a phone in like *Call Nick Ross*

What you have learnt

1 *How to use a survey technique to explore media usage and to present your findings.*

2 *Something about the structure of radio broadcasting in Great Britain.*

3 *Some of the conventions of radio programmes.*

4 *How radio stations seek to create and maintain their audiences.*

Looking and listening: the world of film

In recent years film has become popular again. The slump in cinema audiences in the 1960s and 1970s, combined with the closure of lots of local cinemas, has been reversed as most major towns now have successful multiplexes. The major target audience for the film production companies is 14–24 year olds, so you will probably already have a good knowledge of films through local cinemas and cinema complexes, television screenings or rented videos. This unit seeks to build on that knowledge and open up some new areas for you. This often means giving new names to things you are aware of already.

Film narrative

Most of the films you see tell stories. You know lots of stories because you have seen lots of films. You probably talk to your friends about the films you have seen and when you do it is likely that you will spend a lot of time on the story. We all like to watch good stories to see what will happen next.

ACTIVITY

Everyone knows the story of *Beauty and the Beast*; try retelling the story in groups to refresh your memory.

Once you are clear about the story, make a six-frame **storyboard** of the main events. If you are not sure about storyboards, there is one to help you in Chapter 9 (Figure 9.1). You will also find help on different kinds of shots.

There are several points you need to think about, including:

- what angles and shots you will use (e.g. close-up, long-shot)
- what details you will have in the background
- whether all the pictures will be neutral or whether some will be from a character's **point of view**.

When you have finished this task, you will have learnt quite a lot about film language. All the decisions you have made come under one heading in film criticism, ***mise en scène***. This simply means something which has been deliberately put into the frame (the camera's eye). *Mise en scène* includes:

- angles
- shots
- costume
- scenery.

Props

Props are also an important part of storytelling. Here are a couple of our favourite uses of props. Do you remember the bit in *The Raiders of the Lost Ark* where Harrison Ford is faced by the Arab who swirls his sword around and he shoots the Arab? Or when Luke Skywalker fights with

the laser in *Star Wars*? What are your favourite uses of props?

Look again at your storyboard and see how you have used props in your narrative. You may like to change them over and get feedback from each other. Add any details that you think would make filming easier.

Order of events

In making your storyboard, did you feel that any essentials of the story were left out? You might feel that the storyboard should have dealt with the curse on the Beast or that Beauty's early life could have been built up. The prejudice of the townspeople might have been an important part of the story for your version.

FIG 1.8 *A film version of* Beauty and the Beast *made by the French director Jean Cocteau. What do you think is happening in this scene?*

You need to understand that the order of events in a story does not have to be the same as that shown in a film narrative. Aspects can be changed to give the film a specific emphasis. For example, the famous story *Robin Hood* has the following order of events:

- Robin Hood's childhood as Robin of Locksley
- His teenage years
- Years in which he may have left England to fight in The Crusades
- His battles with the Sheriff of Nottingham
- The forming of the Merry Men
- The adventures
- Return of Richard the Lionheart
- Robin Hood's later years
- His children.

This is an order of events as they might have happened, but a film can start or finish where it chooses. For example, the Kevin Costner version starts in The Crusades and finishes with the return of Richard the Lionheart. The Disney animated version starts with Robin as a young man. In *Robin and Marion*, Sean Connery plays Robin in old age. Do you know any other versions?

So although all the films stem from the same basic story, each film takes a different stance and organises the story differently. The order of events can be jumbled up in a film to make it more interesting. What will the next version be, do you think? How many other stories do you know which have different versions?

ACTIVITY

THE RETURN OF BEAUTY AND THE BEAST

Divide into groups of two or three and take each storyboard of *Beauty and the Beast* in turn. Cut out the six pictures and order them in the following ways:

1. F + A + B + C + D + E
2. E + D + C + A + B + F
3. D + A + B + C + E + F

Try to think of ways in which the scenes can be linked, using some of the techniques listed below or some of your own:

- voice-over
- flashback
- point-of-view shots.

You may need to discuss the meaning of the terms with your teacher. You may also add extra frames in order to make sense of the narrative.

The order in which you see a story is governed by the way a film is cut and put together; in other words by the order of the frames. This is sometimes called **montage**, because that word suggests a film is built up out of smaller fragments. A story can begin and end at any point in a narrative. For example, crime films often start with the discovery of a body and then work backwards in the investigation to find the criminal. We only find out what really happened in the last part of the film. Now paste up your favourite version of the storyboard, adding extra scenes or linking frames so that your version of the story is enjoyable for you.

Whose story is it?

Mostly the camera is an invisible spectator, although some films like *Lady in the Lake* (a 1940s detective story) use the camera as though it were a hero so that the camera gets punched and kissed! In this film, we see the hero only when he looks in a mirror.

Most films are not so extreme, but they often use devices to focus our attention on one character's story more than another's. For example, voice-over controls what we are looking at by giving us one person's point of view about people and events. Even within films we sometimes get point-of-view shots, where for a few moments we see the action as the character would.

Look at your storyboard:

- Does it give more of one person's viewpoint than another's?
- Is this a film about Beauty, about the Beast, or both of them?
- Are there any adjustments you want to make at this stage?

ACTIVITY

SHOT MAKING

Use a video camera/viewfinder to:

1. show Beauty crying
2. show the Beast from behind looking at Beauty
3. show a two-second dialogue in which Beauty and the Beast say hello
4. show Beauty looking down some steps
5. show the Beast waving goodbye.

MAKING SOUND

Use a video camera or audio-cassette to record a sound effect/piece of music to go with each segment.

Stars

From the beginning of film marketing, film-makers realised the power of star images in selling films. Everyone has favourite film stars and they play an important role in a film's narrative. Casting particular stars is a way of getting us involved in the story because their star images carry characteristics we recognise and expect.

ACTIVITY

Discuss the following questions with a partner:

1. Do you both have a favourite star? Why do you like that star?
2. What characteristics do you associate with the following stars?
    - **(a)** Keanu Reeves
    - **(b)** Winona Ryder
    - **(c)** Tom Hanks
    - **(d)** Drew Barrymore

There are many reasons why we like certain stars. They may share our characteristics or have characteristics we would like, or we may just find them attractive. How important is it for people in your group to know who is starring in a film?

ACTIVITY

Discuss in groups what kind of film you would expect to see if you heard that the following were in a film:

- Jim Carrey
- Jodie Foster
- Arnold Schwartzenegger
- Julia Roberts

Many stars are associated with particular parts: they may change their roles in films, but it is hard to change an image.

ACTIVITY

Think about who you would choose for the main parts of *Beauty and the Beast* in a new feature version. Jot down notes about the reasons for your choices and what the actors could bring to the parts. Be prepared to speak about your choices. Compare them with those of the rest of the group and then the group can vote on the casting they want.

Genre

Another marketing element is the genre of a film. Genre is a term which simply means the type of story being told. Typical film genres include westerns, romances, musicals and horror.

When we see an example of one of these films, we know what type of story it is because we recognise:

- the sorts of characters involved
- the settings
- the plots
- the props
- the minor characters.

It is because we recognise these patterns that we can anticipate how the story might develop. For example, if there is a crime committed, we expect the detective to investigate it.

In the Disney version of *Beauty and the Beast* there are references to several genres. The characters sing so it has musical characteristics; there are images from horror films like the gates of the Beast's castle; and, of course, there are elements of romance.

ACTIVITY

In pairs, think about a new version of *Beauty and the Beast* which is to be filmed by a major studio.

❶ Decide on a cast list, compromising if necessary on your original choices.

❷ Design a poster to advertise the film. This should highlight the stars, give the genre the film will concentrate on, and make a key statement or ask a teasing question about the film narrative.

FIG 1.9 *Here is a teaser poster for a new version of the film* Beauty and the Beast, *drawn by a student. Think of a slogan*

From this introductory work you can see that narrative in films is a complicated business and when we watch a film we are using sophisticated skills to follow the story.

What you have learnt

1 *Some film language:* mise en scène, *shots, point of view, montage.*

2 *The story in a film can be constructed in different ways.*

3 *The term narrative refers not only to the events in the story but also to the ways these are linked.*

4 *The selection of stars who will play the characters is an important aspect of the way a film is marketed.*

5 *The genre is an important element in marketing the film.*

6 *Films need an audience, so marketing is an essential activity.*

Further thoughts

In this chapter you have started to examine three major media forms: photography, radio and film. All media forms use certain codes to create meaning, based on conventions and rules. You experience the signs in the media form and use the conventions and rules to interpret them. These allow us to understand the media, because the ways in which they organise their products are based on rules and conventions which we accept. They are the means by which the different media communicate with us, and are often called **media language**. We mostly take this organisation for granted unless a media text draws our attention to the way it breaks the conventions and rules. Students of the media must be prepared to question the organisational codes to get at the meaning. This activity is sometimes called **deconstructing** the media

form or text. To study media forms you must identify how meanings are constructed by media producers and how you and others reconstruct the meanings. As you have seen, by playing with the codes and conventions we can construct new meanings in very straightforward material such as a single photograph. So you must be on the alert and prepared to question your assumptions.

This chapter also provides a basis for looking at other media organisations and their products. Much of the content and treatment of material in various media organisations is very similar, because most are organised in similar ways. The work on narrative, genre and stars in the film unit will therefore also be useful in studying the conventions of other media products, whilst the information on radio broadcasting will give a useful insight into the activities of other media organisations. You must be prepared to build up your knowledge and understanding by making comparisons and looking for similar patterns in other media forms.

Media logs

It is a good idea to keep a media log in which you talk to yourself about media forms. A log is a record of your thinking which allows you the freedom to review your responses and ideas. The most important part of this is that it is *your* thinking that you are concerned with. You might want to think about a film you have seen which you really enjoyed, a news item which really upset you, or an issue reported in the media that you feel strongly about. It does not have to be about your school work. If you decide to do this, here are a few guidelines to help you:

1 Write regularly; specified times in the week are best.
2 Be honest. Sometimes things you come across or ideas you have will be hard to pin down into words. You don't have to have answers and you might finish up with more questions than when you started.
3 Keep your log in a bound notebook or in a separate file on your word processor.
4 Write directly. Don't copy things out which you have written before – your log is not the same as your notes.
5 Date each entry.
6 Use sketches, diagrams, spider diagrams and drawings to help conceptualise your ideas.
7 Jot down plot outlines/sequences, ideas for programmes, design ideas, etc. Work at your skills as there are a whole range of skills and competencies which require good ideas to work.

The log could be the start of the rest of your life!

Here are some questions which might get you going. Use these only if you really do not know where to start.

● Is it true that the camera never lies?
● What makes a good film: the story; the narrative; the star?
● How does radio get over the fact that it is a blind medium?
● What do you want from media studies?

Media representations

Representing the environment

Young markets

Recent surveys in teenage magazines and on BBC's *Newsround* have found that although young people tend to be uninterested in politics, they are concerned about environmental issues. In this unit we will look at how this issue is represented in the media.

Pressure groups like Friends of the Earth, Greenpeace and the World Wildlife Fund have all raised expectations in media consumers. As well as producing colourful and carefully worded material of their own, such groups help to create public opinion, raising the consciousness of audiences so that they begin to seek out products which use less packaging or are not tested on animals. The materials they produce offer a viewpoint or a particular way of seeing the issues involved.

ACTIVITY

Read the article on 'eco-pests' which has been reproduced from *The Daily Telegraph* newspaper (Figure 2.1 on pages 22–3).

Split into groups, then carry out the following tasks:

❶ Make a list of the kinds of activities that the young people are introducing to try to improve the environment.
❷ By looking at the words, picture and tone, discuss what viewpoint the newspaper is taking towards the young people.
❸ Survey the members of your group to find out if any of the issues you listed in 1 are considerations they make when buying products. Add any extra environmental issues which emerge.

Green issues in advertising

Advertising is particularly quick to respond to consumer issues. As a group, try to draw up a list of advertisements from memory which deal with environmental issues. You should then look through magazines to find examples of these concerns. This checklist will be useful as a guide:

● use of words such as natural
● use of colours such as green, blue or white
● references to old, organic or clean production processes
● connotations of health and cleanliness.

Look at Figure 2.2 on page 24. It would be useful if you could bring in any Body Shop or Boots products, packaging or advertising leaflets. All the material you have collected could then be used to create a striking montage, demonstrating the key role played by environmental issues in modern advertising.

ACTIVITY

MAKING ADVERTISEMENTS

You should be aware of some of the ways in which environmental issues are used in advertising. You can now carry out this practical project, either as an individual or with a partner. Try to present your work as neatly and carefully as possible. If you or your partner lack confidence in drawing, you should try to take photographs or use a montage from other sources. At the end of the project you will be asked to make an oral presentation to the group, so you will need to ensure your project is clear and well labelled. Remember that the audience will judge the appearance of the product as well as your presentation.

Brief

Create a new range of perfume/deodorant/ shampoo for young, environmentally conscious teenagers like the ones in the article.

Method

❶ You need to create a portfolio in which you will present the following items:
- sketches of products and their packaging (or you could make mock-ups of the products); name the product and design an overall logo/name for the range
- a full-page advertisement for a specified magazine or comic, plus a letter to that outlet suggesting a placement for the product within the publication
- a storyboard for a television advertisement, plus a letter to a television channel suggesting placement for the product. You may also prepare a short radio advertisement for a commercial radio station.

❷ You may write to Friends of the Earth or some other body for information.
❸ Write a memo to the head of an advertising agency outlining what you have done, giving reasons and evaluating your product.
❹ Role play your ideas to the client in a face-to-face meeting.

To do this activity you have had to go through the production process of an advertising agency. You have carried out all the jobs which are normally specialised. Look at the following list in pairs and see if you know or can guess the nature of the various roles.

- product designer
- image creator
- graphic artist
- photographer
- copywriter
- space buyer
- finance consultant
- jingle writer
- director
- actor.

How many of them did you need to take on in order to complete the task? Did you have a favourite job?

As you have found out, creating a media product is usually a team effort. By experimenting with images and how to present them, you have also learnt about the process of making media products.

Running a campaign

Environmental groups like Greenpeace and Friends of the Earth do not just produce short-lived advertisements; they want to encourage long-term commitment. In order to do this they need to constantly update their material and to use radio, posters, leaflets and free news coverage in order to keep their ideas before the pub dults are unwise to try drinking water from the tap while Carmen Glatt is around. Carmen is only eleven but nobody could question her clarity of vision or her determination. She is very aware that all the water we drink is recycled, says her mum, and she is convinced that anything which comes out of a tap must be polluted in some way. She conscientiously changes the family's water filter every week.

"If someone gets a drink of water from the tap she says 'No, No, No' and throws it away and gets some from the filter. She washes all salad and fruit with filtered water," says her mother. As a nurse, Mrs. Glatt is no slouch on health matters but she admits she is no match for her daughter.

"At school or in someone else's house she is very concerned that the water is not really clean. I tell her that once in a while it's not terrible to drink it and that it can be rude to refuse water in someone else's house." But Carmen is clearly not convinced.

And it is not just the water. There is air pollution too. "She even bought a breathing filter for her father for when he cycles to work," says Mrs. Glatt, clearly both overwhelmed and impressed by her daughter's tenacity. "And he has to buy unleaded petrol," she adds.

When it comes to shopping Carmen accompanies her mother to the supermarket to supervise the family purchases. "She reads the packages of everything and watches out for certain chemicals or artificial sweeteners. She won't have certain kinds of apples because she says they taste of chemicals. She acts as my conscience. I feel like Pinocchio sometimes. She's definitely the driving force for greenness in the family."

The day

Mrs. Glatt is not the only parent in such a position. Once it was pressure groups who pushed concern for the environment. Nowadays it is the nation's children. Litter, endangered species, recycling, fur coats, the ozone layer, trees and unleaded petrol are all concerns for Carmen and her friends at school.

They are entirely typical of children throughout the country, according to Nicky Carter of the Worldwide Fund for Nature (WWF) whose job is to answer as many as 200 letters a day from children.

Clearly they have a lot on their minds. "I'm worried about everything really," concludes Carmen. Indeed she is. "Once," she adds thoughtfully, "I stepped on an insect. I tried to do an operation on it but it died."

Action not words is the order of the day. Most of it is less ambitious than surgery on squashed insects but it is no less committed. Nine-year-old Ben Parker has told his mother that he expects a 'garbageless lunch' — his lunchbox is to contain nothing that cannot be re-used or recycled. But he has already gone a stage further. "He has now decided that re-using and recycling are not good enough. We have to reduce the amount we use," says his mother. She is a keen environmentalist herself but cannot compete with her son. "I make compromises but he carries everything to extremes."

A number of Ben's schoolfriends put out separate bags for the dustbinmen containing only paper. Lisa Wood says, "I taped a great big notice to the bags saying "To be Recycled' but they didn't take any notice. They just chucked them into the lorry along with everything else."

Carmen had tried something similar herself. "My Dad gets lots of newspapers and magazines," she tells her schoolmates." I gave him a plastic carrier bag to put them in so they could be recycled. But he said he wasn't having an old Tesco bag in his office." Josephine Alexander went one stage further. "I got separate bags for each kind of rubbish. But my Dad threw them out. He said they were cluttering up the garage."

The children all nodded wisely at this evidence of the inconsistency and treachery of the adult world. "With people like that you just have to go on and on until they change," says Jessica Tansig with all the wisdom of a 10-year-old veteran.

FIG 2.1

Don't bin it, recycle it: the Glatts go green, policed by children Jonathan and Carmen. 'I feel like Pinocchio', says Mrs Glatt

The most zealous crusaders for the green cause are now children. They tell PAUL VALLELY how they make their families toe the line

e Eco-Pests

Josephine's father, John Alexander, wearily pleads guilty. "She labels me as environmentally unfriendly. She tells us off if she sees aerosols in the house which are not ozone-friendly. It's a constant issue in the household now."

Occasionally he resists. One evening Mrs. Alexander appeared in a fur coat and Josephine protested loudly. "She was eating chicken at the time, so I pointed that out to her," he recalls. However, he was quickly silenced by his wife who feared that the child would stop eating meat.

Mrs. Alexander is, in any case, more responsive. "My purchasing has changed considerably," she admits. "I won't buy shampoo that has been tested on animals. There's no point having a row with her every time I wash her hair." She buys ecologically-sound washing powder too. Throughout the land parents are bullied by their eco-pest children to buy recycled paper, mercury-free batteries and ozone-friendly sprays.

"Our eating habits have changed too," says Mrs. Alexander. But she does not mind being nagged. "It's good that she feels so strongly and it's good that she pushes me. And I don't wear the fur coat now."

The concern over fur is one which Josephine shares with her schoolfriends. "My mother has a mink coat and a fox thing that goes around her neck," says Lisa. "But if she wears it I feel ashamed. I have to tell her."

Organisations like the WWF do their best to harness such enthusiasm and to develop it. "But they need to be wary of simply exploiting sentimental reactions," says Peter Martin of the WWF. "The environmental movement has been very guilty. It's easy to make children think that it is wicked to shoot elephants. But that is not education. You've got to ask why people are poor in Africa and start from there. Children have to learn that there are pressures which make people behave as they do."

Josephine Alexander is already beginning to understand those pressures. "I use too many plastic folders for my school projects," she says, by way of a true confession. "The trouble is you get marks for good presentation."

Logo suggests open mind to experiences

Like a travel logo; we can travel through the product

Luxurious vegetation; secrets of the jungle or rainforest

Face of woman turned away: does not care if we look at her; does not invite our gaze; is indifferent

Nakedness is natural not displayed

EXPLORE
NEW
CULTURES
Go Global

GLOBAL
COLLECTION

Exotic plants suggest nature; plants come from natural products

Ethnic figure suggests beauty, dignity, natural

Label tells us where to buy

Name suggests worldwide

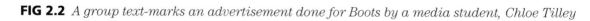

FIG 2.2 *A group text-marks an advertisement done for Boots by a media student, Chloe Tilley*

Ways to help

Greenpeace

Join Greenpeace Frontline

In 1995, membership of Greenpeace Frontline passed the 4,000 mark. Greenpeace Frontliners make regular monthly payments of £10 or more and support Greenpeace's priority campaigns. In return Frontline members get videos, special campaign briefings, a free subscription to Greenpeace Business and a behind-the-scenes look at Greenpeace.

Frontline members have also taken part in direct actions - for instance the invasion of Sellafield at Easter - and offered their professional services free of charge. Actor and singer Jerome Flynn, who is a Frontliner, has generously donated the royalties of his No.1 single, 'Unchained Melody' to Greenpeace.

As a Frontline supporter you would also benefit from an 'inside view' of Greenpeace, getting behind the scenes of campaigns through video updates and background information. For more information on Greenpeace Frontline and how to join, simply complete and return the coupon on this page or call the Frontline phone line: 0171-359 7071.

Include a legacy to Greenpeace in your Will

A Will not only enables you to make provision for people and causes you cared for in your lifetime; it's the only way to ensure that your money and property doesn't end up in the coffers of the government of the day to spend as they see fit.

A legacy to Greenpeace will allow us to carry on our campaigning for the protection of the natural world in your name . For more information on how to include a legacy to Greenpeace in your Will, return the coupon on this page or ring Jan Chisholm on 0171-354 9670.

Join your local group

All around the UK there are groups of people who play an active role in supporting Greenpeace's international campaigns. Greenpeace local groups campaign and take part in direct action against those responsible for damaging the environment and are at the forefront of our activity. To find out where your nearest group is, call Greenpeace on 0171-354 5100.

FIG 2.3

Fruit Market, Ivory Coast   Simon Counsell

Amazonia holds one
in five of all bird
species on Earth.

■

A four mile patch of
rainforest could
contain up to 1,500
species of flowering
plants, 750 species
of tree, 400 of birds,
150 of butterflies,
152 of mammals,
100 of reptiles and
50 of amphibians.

■

An area of tropical
rainforest equivalent
to six football
pitches is destroyed
each minute.

Rainfor
climates. T
and slowly
water back
evapo-trans
clouds and
on the wate
Rainfor
often fragile
from the su
Soil left
erosion. It
systems, wh
absorbed by
ground, ca
farmers.
Rainfor
Their loss
overall rain
this creates
dioxide is r
warming.

Logging in Gabo

THE WEALTH OF THE RAINFORESTS

We all benefit from the rainforests' varied resources.
Tropical forest plants have yielded chemicals used in many
forms of western medicine, including treatments for
bronchitis, laryngitis, epilepsy and leukaemia. Seventy per
cent of the 3,000 plants identified by the US National Cancer
Institute as having anti-cancer properties come from the
tropical rainforests.

The industrial world too, has benefitted from rainforest
produce. Rubber is just one of the materials that came
originally from rainforest areas.

Several familiar and important food crops, such as rice,
maize, pineapples, bananas, coffee, avocados and potatoes
were originally from tropical forest plants. We still depend on
the wild ancestors of such plants to improve crop yields and
increase resistance to disease and pests.

Rainforests can be regarded as a vast natural library with
much of the information which they hold still untapped.
Many species of plants and animals will disappear before
scientists have even been able to identify them.

Grey Parrot, Ivory Coast
Simon Counsell

FIG 2.4

EST

e in moderating local
soaking up tropical rain,
ground. Trees also recycle
ugh a process called
from leaves gathers as
han a billion people depend
rainforests.

t of rain, protecting the
ell as shading the ground

have been cleared is liable to
rivers and irrigation
h silt. Instead of being
straight off the hard-baked
evastating effects for local

and sensitive ecosystem.
ns including a reduction in
cleared by burning, and
s of its own since carbon
ere, contributing to global

FACTS

In the Ivory Coast, a forested slope loses only 30 kilograms of soil per hectare per year. A deforested slope loses 138 tonnes.

■

Rainforest burning adds 2.4 billion tonnes of carbon dioxide to the atmosphere every year.

■

The World Bank-funded Balbina dam resulted in the flooding of nearly 2500 square kilometres of tribally inhabited rainforest.

■

On average one tribe has disappeared from Brazil every year this century.

Sally Zalewski / ICCE

RAINFOREST DESTRUCTION

Rainforests have taken as long as 100 million years to evolve but could be destroyed in less than 100 years. The greatest threats are the spread of farming and logging, but development schemes such as dams and mines are also destroying huge areas.

FARMING

Millions of people in tropical countries clear the forests to grow food to eat and sell. In some countries, settlement of forest areas is deliberately encouraged and supported by international aid programmes. The Indonesian Government is moving millions of people from the islands of Java and Bali to the fragile tropical forests of Borneo, Sulawesi and Irian Jaya.

In Latin America, cattle ranchers have cleared vast tracts of forest for pasture. Throughout the tropics, forests have been destroyed to make way for crops of luxury foodstuffs demanded by the western world.

LOGGING

At least 12.5 million acres of tropical forest are affected each year by the commercial timber industry. Although loggers often seek only a few preferred species of the many trees available, even this 'selective logging' can cause immense damage. Felling just one mature hardwood tree can destroy or damage many others, with still more being crushed by logging equipment or cleared to make way for logging roads.

To satisfy international demand for the best tropical hardwoods, the logging industry continues to exploit virgin forest. As loggers drive roads into the forests they open up previously inaccessible areas to land hungry settlers, who may clear the forests permanently.

lic eye. Posters are particularly effective in catching attention.

Figure 2.3 on page 25 shows a page taken from a Greenpeace pamphlet. Discuss whether it is effective in putting a message across.

Campaigning groups use spinoffs such as mugs, T-shirts and badges, not only to raise funds but also as a means of advertising their messages. Such campaigns seek to persuade people using a whole range of emotional and logical techniques.

Look at Figure 2.4 on pages 26–7, a page of a leaflet from Friends of the Earth.
❶ What methods are used to persuade people?
❷ What role is played by the photographs?
❸ What other media products could fit in with this leaflet?
❹ How effective is the leaflet? Does it fulfil its aim?
Now write a critique of the leaflet, using your notes to help you.

You may want to start a campaign of your own using some of the techniques you have come across.

Representations of the environment in films

Concern about the environment has become a theme of many media products and popular film has reflected this concern. Look at the following synopses and see if you can think of any films which fit these plots.

- Animals, or particularly one animal, finds its habitat threatened by man or pollution and has to move, fight or suffer.
- Some man-made danger is being released into the environment, but there is a cover-up. Will the plot be uncovered in time?
- A disaster occurs which sends mankind into a more primitive world.
- Some villain/potential disaster leaves the world teetering on the brink. What will happen?

You probably know quite a few films that fit these scenarios, but could you come up with your own blockbuster? Films are very expensive products and producers need to be convinced that they will have a return for their investment.

Split into teams to compete for financial backing from your teacher, who is now an independent producer with a conscience wanting to make a socially aware film. Prepare your brief and then give an oral presentation. Remember you need to sell the idea strongly, so use any persuasive techniques you have learnt. You could aim for a mainstream film for a mass audience or an alternative product for a specified target group. Use the production flow chart in Figure 2.5 to help you plan.

As you will be aware from studying this section, the media are quick to respond to contemporary issues. One of the key questions in media which you should think about is whether they simply *respond* to public opinion or whether they *influence* it.

DECISIONS

You are going to take a story from a well-known book. Perhaps you know a book already or you can pretend that Michael Crichton (*Jurassic Park*, *Congo*) or John Grisham (*The Firm*, *The Client*) has written one. Think of a suitable title.

Stories

You will use an original idea. You want to make a more experimental film; a drama/documentary or an animation version.

PORTFOLIO OUTCOME

Synopsis of plot highlighting the most powerful scenes. You could storyboard one to suggest genre and content.

Stars need to be signed up early but are expensive. For a mainstream film you will need at least two main stars and a support.

Stars

As your project is cheaper you could go for no stars or two cheaper stars in the hope of larger box office returns.

PORTFOLIO OUTCOME

Name your stars and give reasons for choices. The following chart may help.

Star values

Tom Hanks (*Forest Gump*)	Val Kilmer (*Batman Forever*)	Bob Hoskins (*Roger Rabbit*)
Tom Cruise (*Interview with a Vampire*)	Dustin Hoffman (*Outbreak*)	Sam Neill (*Jurassic Park*)
Nicole Kidman (*To Die For*)	Bridget Fonda (*The Assassin*)	Laura Dern (*Jurassic Park*)
Jodi Foster (*Silence of the Lambs*)	Emma Thompson (*Junior*)	Holly Hunter (*The Piano*)

You will choose a director who is successful at the moment.

Director

You may decide to choose yourself as director, to work as a team or to go for someone less well known.

PORTFOLIO OUTCOME

You should name your director and give reasons for your choice.

You will need a big star to sell your film.

Music

You should go for an indie band.

PORTFOLIO OUTCOME

You should write reasons for your choice. Make a short tape of sample music to use at your oral presentation.

You should prepare a teaser poster to let the public know the film is coming.

Poster

You will need to produce a teaser poster early on to attract interest in the film.

PORTFOLIO OUTCOME

A mock-up poster.

You are now ready for the presentation and should remember to use any relevant environmental or other contemporary issues as selling points.

FIG 2.5 *Production flow chart*

What you have learnt

❶ *Non-fictional texts and fictional texts both represent issues, but in different ways.*

❷ *Current issues are reflected in the media.*

❸ *Media work is very rarely the work of a single gifted individual.*

❹ *Media organisations are always looking at new ways of representing issues.*

Representing gender

In Chapter 1 we looked briefly at stereotyping and how images can be used to represent people to different audiences. But language too is important. The words that we use to describe people and objects can also lead to assumptions being made about individuals or groups of people.

- Why are ships and cars often referred to as 'she'?
- Do they have feminine attributes?
- Or, historically, were they driven and captained by men who were therefore in control of them?
- What other objects are given the pronoun 'he' or 'she'?
- Can you think of any reasons why this should be?

Words can be very powerful. Language acts as a sort of code; it not only gives a meaning which we have all learnt to understand but also imposes a kind of value structure on whatever is being represented.

For instance, if in the media women are con-stantly referred to as 'slim', 'beautiful', 'mother-to-be' and 'wife', whilst men are described as 'athletic', 'strong', 'hard working' and 'success-ful', we can easily begin to assume that a woman's role is one of carer and object of (male) desire, and a male's role is one of protec-tor (to women) and provider. But is that really how people want to be represented?

ACTIVITY

Look at the sentences below. What kinds of people do you think they describe?
(a) This person stays at home during the day and takes care of the children.
(b) This person likes to spend the weekend maintaining the motorbike.
(c) These children all hope to become doctors.
(d) This person is a chef.
Now study the photographs of these people (Figure 2.6a–d) on page 32. How accurate were you?

Did you make the mistake of assuming that people who look after children are women and those who ride and maintain motorbikes are men? Were you guilty of stereotyping people according to their preconceived gender roles? If you were, you were not alone. It happens all the time in the media.

ACTIVITY

See what other people think. Try the same exercise on a sample of people – about ten should be enough to give you a reasonable response to analyse. Think carefully about the survey instrument.

What conclusions can you draw from your survey about the way in which people stereotype others by their verbal descriptions?

If we make generalisations about others from verbal descriptions we have been given, imagine how mass audiences will react, even sub-consciously, to output from the media. In a recent article in a quality newspaper a female politician was described, in the middle of a political article, as having an 'English rose complexion'. Many media analysts think that this kind of description is unnecessary, because it is irrelevant to the report being written and therefore trivialises it.

What do you think?

ACTIVITY

Try this exercise to look at the language used in newspapers to describe men and women. Divide into groups; each group should analyse a different paper. You could use the following headings to collate your findings:
- name of paper
- article headline
- page number

- reference to men
- reference to women.

What conclusions can you draw from this study?

Magazines

Magazine titles often help with the identification of the target audience.

ACTIVITY

WHAT'S IN A NAME?
Look at the list of potential magazine titles below and, with a partner, describe the target audience for each one:
- Tea Break
- Mama Mia!
- Business Executive
- Hollywood
- Spanner
- Needle and Thread
- Monsieur
- Tiara

Now, select one of the titles and decide what types of articles you would expect to find in the magazine. It would be a good idea to split up the titles amongst the group. When you have decided upon this, design a contents page for the magazine, thinking carefully about both the images and the language that you need to use in order to appeal to your target audience. Your finished pages could be used to form a classroom display on language and representations.

We expect that in order to accomplish this task you found yourselves categorising your audiences and presenting stereotypical images and articles to them. You can see that the media do have a problem. In order to reach a specific audience they generally present the same range of stereotypes. It is quite difficult to present something new.

FIG 2.6

(a) *This person stays at home during the day and takes care of her children*
(b) *This person likes to spend the weekend maintaining her motorbike*
(c) *This person is a chef*
(d) *These children all hope to become doctors*

MAKING MAGAZINES

You work for a well-known magazine publishing group who are responsible for a number of popular titles. They now wish to launch a new magazine on to the market aimed at a mixed gender teenage audience (14–17 years). They don't want to make it a subject specific magazine (e.g. only music), but want to include a range of articles and features. Your task is to produce a front cover and a sample article covering a double page for their first edition.

Method

❶ Conduct a survey amongst a group of teenagers who would be part of the target group. A sample of eight to ten would be sufficient, but they obviously need to be of both genders. Remember, you are trying to find out what kinds of articles and features they would like to see in a magazine, so you will need to ask carefully constructed questions. Perhaps you will give them a range of examples to choose from.

❷ Collate your answers and decide which articles you will include. This should give you a good idea of the type of magazine you are producing.

❸ Select a title.

❹ Design and produce the front cover: sketch a **mock-up** first, thinking carefully about the layout. Consider appropriate language, images and colour.

❺ Select one of the articles for your double-page spread; write the text, design the layout and produce it.

❻ Finally you will need to produce a report outlining the choices you have made, identifying any problems you have encountered and evaluating your final production.

Television: soap operas

Soap operas are quite clearly one of the most popular of all of the television genres.

- What programmes do you watch?
- Why do you like them?

Some people like watching them because of the storylines, others because they like the characters. An American study undertaken by D. H. Meehan identified several different roles allocated to women in American soap operas and dramas. They include:

- **The good wife.** This character is quite domestic and home-centred. She does not appear to have a role outside the family home – this she leaves to her husband.
- **The victim.** This character is very passive and tends to attract disasters to her – whether they are accidental or violent.
- **The harpy.** This character is an aggressive single woman; quite powerful. She is not afraid to chase men.

How accurate do you think these descriptions are for British soaps? Can you give some examples from existing programmes that would fit these definitions? Can you think of other definitions that you could add to this list?

In pairs, compile a list of male character types, giving examples from a range of programmes. The first one has been done for you.

- **The wide-boy:** like Steve MacDonald from *Coronation Street* or Ian Beale from *EastEnders*.

The character types that we see in soap operas generally have specific functions; the stereotypical situations that the characters find themselves in help to advance the narrative of the programmes. Write a brief character profile for a character from your favourite soap opera. What future storylines would you expect to find him or her in?

Obviously, certain characters behave in certain ways. Once you know them, they can be really quite predictable.

Look at the profiles below. What existing soap operas do you think these characters would fit in to?

❶ Female: a single professional woman; bright and ambitious.

❷ Male: mid 40s, single parent with three daughters. Moved in to the area to manage the local post office. This is a career change – our character had previously been in the police.

❸ Male: late teens; studying 'A' levels at college – keen to go to university to study medicine. Family supportive but lack the finances to help.

❹ Female: late 70s; widow with no visible family. Active retired health visitor.

❺ Couple: mid 20s; African ethnic origin. Female works in a bank, male is a primary school teacher. They have decided to establish their careers before beginning a family.

❻ Family: parents late 30s; father a long distance lorry driver, mother intends to run a small knitting business from home. Eldest child (male: mid teens) keen on motorbikes; middle child (female: early teens) wants to be a nurse; youngest child (female: 8 years) disabled and attends a local special school. Good family relationships.

In pairs, **script** and storyboard the scenes which introduce two of these characters/groups into the soap. In order to do this properly you will need to expand the profile. Give names to the characters and work out more background details about them; then you will need to decide upon a suitable storyline which would identify them as future central characters.

You will see from the profiles that most of these characters have very positive attributes, and if you look at the characters in existing soap operas many of them have too. Of course, for the sake of a good or dramatic story negative events occur – marriages and relationships which appear to be stable break up, teenagers who appear to be well balanced hit the drug scene – but in general stereotypes are often pos-itive and are employed in order to help us, the audience, identify with the characters being presented.

In pairs, select four characters from existing soap operas and list their positive attributes. Give an oral feedback of your findings to the rest of the class.

Launching a new soap opera

A new soap opera needs to be carefully marketed in order to attract an audience. Too much advertising hype can, however, put people off or lead them to expect more than the programme has to offer.

In 1992 the BBC launched a new soap opera called *Eldorado*. It was set amongst a British community living in Spain: a new and original idea with exciting possibilities. However, the programme never lived up to its pre-production hype and it was withdrawn after a very short time. Although there were several factors that led to the programme's final downfall, this case does highlight the problems of advertising a new programme: too little and people simply don't tune in, but too much information may lead to expectations that can't be met.

Look at the programme outline opposite and, in a small group, decide how you would market this programme to a prospective audience.

You can make your soap opera either a radio or a TV production. You might like to consider some of the following promotional ideas:
- trailers
- articles in programme listings magazines
- tabloid articles
- photo-calls for the 'stars'
- billboard adverts.

Programme outline
Scheduled: Monday and Friday, BBC at 7 p.m.
Name: Greenlawns
Location: A new estate on the edge of a large city built on the site of an old golf course. Mixed range of housing. Small precinct of shops including a grocers, post office, bank, hairdressers and a pub.
Character profiles: Use the range provided earlier and add new sets of your own for the pub owners and the hairdressers.
Opening episode: The opening of the new pub – an opportunity for characters to introduce themselves and for you to establish a range of narratives which link the characters and give a sense of dramatic realism.

Method
❶ Decide on the new character profiles.
❷ Decide on the outline for the first episode.
❸ Select the main narrative strands and the lead characters you wish to highlight in your publicity material.
❹ Finally, produce a range of promotional materials. Individually, you will need to keep a log of the work you have done so that you can write a report and evaluation at the end.

What you have learnt

❶ *You have developed your understanding of an important media concept: stereotyping. Stereotypes can be positive and negative.*

❷ *Language is an important element in representing our attitudes to people and things.*

❸ *Our attitudes very often affect the ways in which we see things. If our attitudes change then the way we see things changes.*

❹ *Viewpoint is a central media concept.*

Representing the real world

Do you believe everything you hear on the news, see in the television or read in the newspapers? As you have seen, meanings can be changed according to how material is organised and presented. So we hope that by now you will be saying 'Probably not, because it depends on how

FIG 2.7 *Deciding priorities – the story*   © *MEW*

FIG 2.8 *Deciding priorities – the photographs*   © *MEW*

the real world is presented to us'. This unit asks you to examine in more detail how events in the world are presented and the different techniques used.

ACTIVITY

A. WHAT IS NEWS?

In pairs, decide if these stories are news stories.

❶ Your group raises £100 for Save the Children.

❷ Your local area chooses a carnival queen.

❸ There is a new outbreak of violence in Bosnia.

❹ England win a cricket test series.

❺ The Prime Minister resigns.

❻ A small village in Nigeria gets a new school.

B. WHO DECIDES WHAT THE NEWS WILL BE?

In groups, try to find out what newspapers, radio and television bulletins other members of the group have looked at or listened to in the past week. Can they remember any stories? Why do they remember those particular stories?

C. HOW IS THE NEWS GATHERED?

Study Figure 2.9, a story about some exam students which appeared in a local evening newspaper in South Wales.

❶ Who was involved? Where did it happen? At what time did the event take place?

❷ How did the newspaper find out about the story?

❸ How many people were interviewed? Did the reporter(s) phone these people or go to see them?

This was a fairly simple news item and it was relatively easy for the reporter to gather and present the information.

These activities are trying to make you think about the importance of the audience. All news organisations must present stories that the audience needs to feel informed about; otherwise they will not have an audience. Newspapers need to increase their circulation; television and radio stations aim to increase their share of the audience. News values are defined by what news organisations think are important and acceptable to their target audience. Different news organisations have different news agendas. Do any news organisations set up an agenda of topics which interests you?

Exam students stuck

STUDENTS sitting crucial exams were among hundreds of victims of a huge traffic snarl-up in Swansea's Eastside yesterday.

Most were on buses clogged in a morning rush-hour traffic jam which stretched from the city centre to Morfa.

West Glamorgan County Council turned off the lights at one of Swansea's busiest junctions for important work to them — but failed to give any warning through the media.

It meant hundreds of unsuspecting motorists were caught. Bus drivers alerted bosses at South Wales Transport control of the plight of worried students on board.

The bus company rang Swansea College and explained why some exam candidates would be late, said SWT general manager Peter Heath. "It was absolute chaos with buses half-an-hour late coming in." He criticised the council for failing to tell the company or the public that the traffic lights

at Parc Tawe were being shut down for the day.

Council contractors Peek Traffic Services had to switch the signals off from early morning to replace the entire control system.

Mr Heath said: "What we find annoying and frustrating is that the county council's PR, or lack of it, when it comes to implementing them is appalling."

The council offered no apology for its failure to warn people. "But we did notify AA Road Watch," said a spokeswoman. "It had to be shut down sometime. Yesterday was as problematic as any other," said a senior county engineer.

Around 400 students were due to sit GCSEs, A-levels, City and Guilds and B.Tech exams at the Tycoch college.

Vice-principal Malcolm Charnley said: "Students arriving late for examinations had the requisite amount of time allocated to them so they were not disadvantaged in any way."

FIG 2.9

ACTIVITY

❶ Closeness to home. Have a look back at your answers to Activity A. Choose an appropriate audience for each story and an appropriate media organisation which would publish or broadcast such a story.

❷ Content. Have a look back at your answers to Activity B. How might media organisations interest young people in the news?

❸ Angle and treatment. Look back at your answers to Activity C. In what way has the narrative been constructed? (Remember the narrative is more than the story.) Here are some questions to help:

- Who is the suffering hero?
- Who helps the hero?
- Who is the enemy?
- Is there a happy ending?
- Do any of the words dramatise the story?
- Who will the editorial blame for the incident?

Can you make a new narrative? You could either reorganise the paragraphs as you did for *Beauty and the Beast* or make up some interviews with the parents or the students themselves and construct a new narrative, using some of the original material.

Television news

Television news organisations want to encourage viewers to feel that they are being informed and entertained in comfortable and familiar ways. So news programmes have familiar conventions: presenters, format, running order. When something is new or unfamiliar, it often causes a great deal of controversy. Can you remember any occasions when a news organisation changed its time-slot, format, presenters and style of presentation?

Television news has four main formats:

1 extended bulletin
2 news summary

3 news flash
4 magazine-type format.

Can you think of an example of each kind? Is there any pattern to the times of transmission?

We will now deconstruct a typical extended news bulletin to show how it is organised by sets of conventions.

The opening title sequence

This has a central function of branding the programme. Branding means giving the programme a recognisable image which is familiar to the viewers. It is, therefore, carefully planned and often updated.

ACTIVITY

❶ Break down an extended bulletin from your early evening news programme into titling, graphics, images, music and sound. How are these combined to represent where you live?

❷ Make up a storyboard for the title sequence of a news programme which would interest young people.

The presenters

These are some of the most well-known faces in the country. They are central to the way the news organisation links to its audience, so they are very carefully chosen. How many news presenters can your group name?

Here are some of the different jobs that modern newsreaders carry out:

- anchoring the news by linking the different stories
- producing the copy of the story
- carrying out on-air interviews.

Often newsreaders become media personalities in their own right and appear in other media productions. Can you think of any?

ACTIVITY

Choose a newsreader who is well known in your area. In pairs, study his or her broadcasting role:
- How does the newsreader dress on-air?
- Does he or she have any kind of accent?
- Does he or she work alone or with co-presenters? What is the relationship/gender balance?
- How many different tasks does he or she carry out on the programme?
- What off-air activities is he or she involved in, if any?
- Would he or she need to change to appear on national television?

Television companies compete for the best presenters and sometimes reshape the whole image of the programme around a single presenter. They sometimes encourage rivalries between different presenters. Can you think of any examples? National news organisations often recruit from regional news organisations.

ACTIVITY

A famous newsreader has defected to a rival news programme. You decide on a revamp of the style of the programme. Write profiles for a new team of presenters thinking about:
- the kind of image you now want
- the representation of gender
- the representation of race.

The running order

The programme editors will meet to discuss the stories as they develop. It is these editors who decide the running order and length of items. They will need advice from reporters, lawyers, presenters and will be working within a programme policy about how to present the stories.

ACTIVITY

In small groups, deconstruct a *News At Ten* bulletin by:
1. listing each item in the order in which it occurs
2. timing the length of the programme and the length of each individual item
3. studying the typical narrative flow:
   - a summary of main items at the beginning
   - number of items before/after the break
   - the trailer for Part 2 at the end of Part 1
   - summary at start of Part 2
   - content of stories in Parts 1 and 2
   - the final story.

When would this typical flow be disrupted?

The lead story

This is the most important item in the programme and always comes first. The lead story can have a number of different parts: location reports, graphics, interviews. These are combined in different ways into an item. The presenter links the different segments together using a script. The script is made up of the words the presenter uses and is usually read from an auto-cue machine which allows the presenter to look directly at the camera. It establishes the who, when and where of the story. The studio setting is important; it is conventional to have graphics of different kinds behind the presenter.

ACTIVITY

MAKING NEWS

In this activity you are the news presenter. You have to read the script from an auto cue with the sound of a news programme turned off at appropriate points. You will need:
1. **An auto cue.** Use two washing up liquid bottles, two knitting needles (30–40 cm long), a strong cardboard box wide enough for the bottles, a strip of paper which is continuous,

scissors and sticky tape. Figure 2.10 shows you how to construct the model.

❷ **A script.** Record a news programme which has been subtitled using Teletext (page 888). Transfer an accurate transcript (a written version of the presenter's words) of the script on to the continuous strip of paper.

Make video recordings of you and a partner each reading the news or particular news items from the auto cue.

The location report

This is probably the most important and expensive segment of the news programme. It is presented by a correspondent who is linked to the studio-based presenter. The job is often the most sought after, as it can mean lots of travel, danger and excitement. Correspondents can be as famous and as visible as presenters. Can you name any?

Here are some things to think about in location reports:

● How and when did the television crew get to the location?
● What does a location report add to a script?
● Does a correspondent just tell you about what has happened?
● What is the relationship between the studio and the correspondent?
● Are some locations used more than others? Why?
● Why might voice-overs be used for some location reports?

You should add your own questions. Remember, the conventions of the location report are developing all the time as technology makes more and more possible.

Graphics

Television emphasises the visual when presenting information. Producers try to work out all sorts of ways to give visual support to spoken

---

ACTIVITY

Look for newsworthy stories to report. Choose one and decide on a suitable location for it. Then write and record a location report for your chosen story. Try to look directly at the camera. Can you still use notes and communicate effectively?

material. Graphics are an essential part of this. They take many forms and are becoming increasingly sophisticated. Many are now animated using the new computer technology.

ACTIVITY

Using any technology you have access to, design and produce suitable graphics for a lead story about:
● children's television viewing habits
● the cost of CDs
● a new breakthrough in the treatment of meningitis.

Interviews

Interviews are a key feature of news presentation on television. Here are the main types:

● live/on the spot
● pre-recorded
● studio based with invited guest, often a key player or an expert
● studio and location based, often now by satellite using split-screen techniques.

Interviews raise a lot of controversial questions in terms of media practices: the interviewer's role; his or her style of questioning; and the balance of the interview. Consider the following:

1 Cut off the top of the box to make a tray. Make two holes large enough for the rods to spin easily. Make sure the holes are placed so that the bottles can spin easily too.

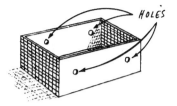

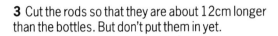

2 Make a hole in the bottom of each bottle and make the hole in the top bigger, so that the rods can be fitted tightly.

3 Cut the rods so that they are about 12cm longer than the bottles. But don't put them in yet.

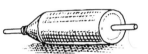

4 Write your news-script on the paper strip (make sure the letters are large enough so that they can be seen by the reader from a distance).

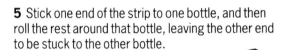

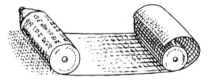

5 Stick one end of the strip to one bottle, and then roll the rest around that bottle, leaving the other end to be stuck to the other bottle.

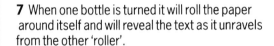

6 Place the bottle 'rollers' inside the box and then push the rods through the holes in the box and the bottles, so that the bottles can rotate on the rods.

7 When one bottle is turned it will roll the paper around itself and will reveal the text as it unravels from the other 'roller'.

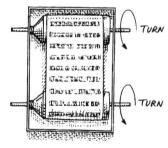

FIG 2.10 *How to make an auto cue*

- Can you think of interviewers who have a very aggressive style of interviewing?
- Do women interview in the same way as men?
- Does the interview allow equal access to different points of view on an issue?
- Are the opinions of some groups rarely represented on television news?

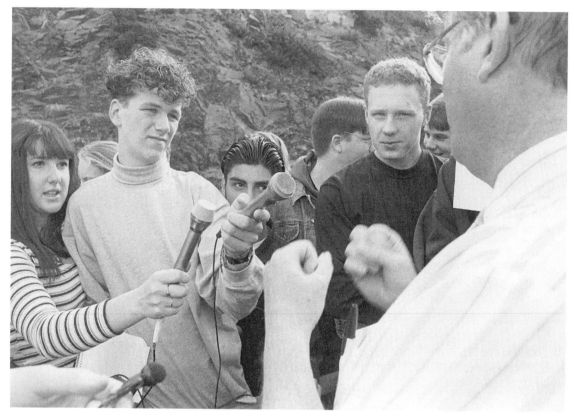

© MEW

FIG 2.11 *News gathering – the media bloodhounds*

Interviewers need to learn how to get accurate and precise information from people. This needs extensive practice. The keys to a good story are the who, what, when and where questions.

ACTIVITY

Your task is to cover a local pollution incident. Fish have been dying and local fishermen have blamed a local factory. In pairs, make a list of the questions you would ask the following people:

- the fisherman who contacted the media
- an official from the Regional Water Authority
- a spokesperson from the local council responsible for environmental health
- the local factory owner
- a local householder.

Dramatise the interviews, taking it in turns to interview and be interviewed. When you are ready, record the interviews on location or in a studio setting.

create comic possibilities. We wait for his reactions. The skill of the comedy script team is to make us wait for the perfect time for our expectations to be met so that they are released in laughter. It seems ridiculous to feel that we should feel guilty because he is a stereotypical grumpy old man or that Del in *Only Fools and Horses* is a wide-boy or Patsy in *Absolutely Fabulous* is a middle-aged leftover from the 1960s. The same can be true for major soap opera characters. Characters, as you have seen in the unit on gender representations, start as stereotypical profiles but slowly become individuals whose lives, loves, problems, successes and failures we follow.

As a consequence, your analysis of stereotypes and stereotyping needs to be handled with care. As a student of the media you need to look carefully at the dominant patterns of representation in our society and to recognise that we accept these views uncritically most of the time. They are how the world is mediated to us. Our views about what it means to be Welsh or northern or black or a woman or a British Asian or a political asylum seeker can be constructed by the media. We should be asking where our views and our images come from, then we can question their validity by reconstructing them. They can also be part of our enjoyment of the media. The key question is, in whose interests is a particular form of representation operating? Often the process can be harmless. At its worst, when it denies other people their humanity, it can have terrible consequences.

3

Media organisations and audiences

Pop programmes on radio and television

Radio

Your earlier work on radio has probably shown you how important a part music can play in your life, especially when you are young. Read this extract from an interview with a middle-aged woman:

❝ When I was 14 in 1964 you couldn't hear the type of music I liked on BBC radio. I was into rhythm and blues and rock music. I remember my parents bought me a transistor radio and this used to pick up Radio Luxembourg which had a different style of presenter. The disc jockeys played rock and roll and Luxembourg was the only station to broadcast the top 20. I didn't have headphones so I used to have it on really low and lie with my ear to it, so the next morning my face was indented with the patterns of the sound box. ❞ **Kim**

When you interviewed older media users in Chapter 1, did they make any comments like these?

Today young listeners have many different stations available which play contemporary music in a wide variety of styles. This is what a modern teenager says about listening habits:

❝ I like a lot of different kinds of music. When I'm doing my homework I like to listen to Red Dragon radio which is our local station. It's good because you hear about things going on in the area and sometimes people you know write in. I like listening to groups like Oasis. The radio does not always play the sorts of music which my friends like such as rave, so we tend to listen to a lot of music on Walkman and I am hoping to have a CD player for my birthday. ❞ **Angela**

These comments remind us how much things have changed. Did you find evidence of this when you surveyed your group's use of radio in Chapter 1?

ACTIVITY

❶ Make your own list of the ways in which technology has changed since the 1960s. You could start with the change in records and use electrical equipment catalogues to help you. Here are some headings:
  ● equipment
  ● product
  ● shops.

❷ Use an appropriate survey technique to find out:
- what channels students use for music listening
- what channels are listened to most
- what programmes are listened to most
- how often students buy records or CDs.

Discuss in a small group the target audience for the favourite programmes and say how this can be determined simply by listening to snatches of the programmes.

Look back at Kim's comments at the beginning of the chapter. We can see the pleasure she had in listening to music. We don't all like the same things and diversification of types of programme has been important in maintaining the audience.

Look at Figure 3.1. What would you add to the music tree? Most of these musical tastes are catered for by radio programmes. You could try to match up programmes to types of music. You could also try to match the programmes to age, as this is a really important category for musical broadcasting.

FIG 3.1

Recently there has been a controversy over the Rolling Stones being played on Radio 2, which has middle-of-the-road tastes. The producer explained that Mick Jagger was now over 50, so many of his fans were middle-aged and more likely to listen to Radio 2 than Radio 1.

ACTIVITY

MAKING A PROGRAMME

Many musical stars span the generations; such as David Bowie, The Beatles and Elvis Presley. Choose a star and make a musical history programme about him or her or a serious analysis of his or her style. You will need snatches of music and a script. Record your programme.

Television

Music on television has given audiences different kinds of pleasures.

ACTIVITY

Working in pairs, jot down how listening to music on radio is different to watching a pop video on television. Here are some categories to get you going:
- locations
- mood
- pictures.

Pop music has had many different programmes which have come and gone, but *Top of The Pops* goes on for ever. Its purpose has always been to show artists whose songs are popular at the moment. In the early days when an artist was not available the programme used dancers to interpret the songs, but nowadays videos can plug that gap. However, the point of the programme is to show stars live in the studio with an audience close to them. Live shows have

FIG 3.2 *Performance with live audience is typical of coverage in pop journalism and TV*

different production problems from pre-recorded shows.

ACTIVITY

EXAMINING *TOP OF THE POPS*

What production problems do you think producing a programme like this involves? Use the credits list to identify:
- the things which need to be done before the programme goes out live, e.g. running order, continuity, research, hiring technicians, contracts, budget, lights, camera angles, studio sets, etc.
- the things you associate with *Top of The Pops*, i.e. its conventions, presenters, audience, etc.

The biggest rival to *Top of The Pops* is *The Chart Show*, which has no presenters and uses videos to show the best-selling singles. Rather than having one chart, *The Chart Show* breaks buying down further into a rock chart and indie chart as well as the overall one. Why does it do this? What effect does it have on the audience?

Making pop programmes

This is a rich area for production. If you decide to make a programme for television or radio, think about:

● the range of music involved
● whether to use a presenter
● the kind of presenter
● the type of programme: live/video, music only or music/talk.

FIG 3.3 *Song lyrics*

FIG 3.4 *CD cover – front and back*

See if you can spot a hole in the market for a more specialist programme aimed at an audience who you may feel is under-represented.

Alternatively you might want to make a pop video. Many famous film directors have enjoyed working with pop videos. Derek Jarman worked with The Pet Shop Boys. Kleinman, the creator of the startling credit sequences for the Bond film *Goldeneye*, has made videos for Madonna, Prince and Van Halen.

What you have learnt

1 Pop music has always meant a great deal to teenagers and reflects their ideas and interests.

2 Pop music is a hybrid term which covers many types of music, each of which has extremely loyal fans. Being a fan makes it hard to see the viewpoint of fans who follow different stars, bands and types of music.

3 Pop music has its own conventions of presentation on radio and on television.

4 There is a strong tradition of live performance in radio and television presentations.

Promoting pop

The popular music business is big business. Most of the records released carry the label of the so-called **majors**. These are companies which are so huge that they not only produce records but also have interests in television, publishing and other leisure industries. The majors include companies like Sony, whose electrical empire spreads throughout the world, even taking in record labels such as Columbia, CBS and Epic. Warner Brothers, once a film studio in Hollywood, now makes television programmes and produces records. Chapter 5 has a unit on another powerful global commercial organisation, Disney Enterprises.

These powerful conglomerates are not the only companies to make records. The alternative to majors are the **indie** companies, which are often very small and therefore do not always last very long because they are prepared to take financial risks. The majors tend to look to indie companies for the new trends and influences, and if a band is successful under an indie label it will soon be pursued by the majors. Television programmes like *The Chart Show* give coverage to the indie top ten and so this is a good place to start asking questions about the majors, independents and indie organisations.

ACTIVITY

In groups, make a list of records which you have bought in the last year and find out what labels the songs were released by.

Stars

These are the most important asset of any recording company. Like film stars, stars of pop music tend to be glittering, untouchable objects of desire. This is why some fans find meeting, touching or getting the autograph of a star completely overwhelming. Richard Dyer has done a great deal of work on film stars and much of what he has written can be applied to the pop world as well.

Names

A star name is very important in the creation of an image and in the past many pop stars have changed their names.

ACTIVITY

Look at the list of pop names below and discuss what impression is created by them:
- Alvin Stardust
- Gary Glitter
- Cliff Richard
- Madonna
- Prince
- Robbie Williams
- Donna Dawson
- Sid Vicious
- Johnny Rotten.

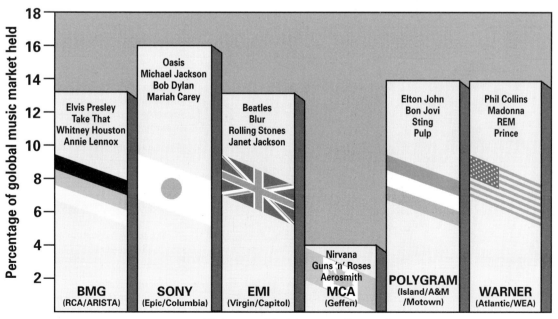

Major worldwide recording artists

FIG 3.5

When stars do not change their names, it may be because their own names suit their image or because they are trying to say something about being ordinary.

Group names are even more important for identifying audiences. Some names can be quite obscure or unusual. For example, the Boo Radleys are named after a character in the novel *To Kill a Mockingbird* who is treated as an idiot but saves the child heroine from attack at the end of the book. Such a name can say a lot about a group. Do they feel misfits; mistreated by society; misunderstood? Are they in touch with the child within them? Are they reaching out to the thousands of students who have read that book for GCSE? Or does it just sound enigmatic? Groups take a long time to decide on their names.

ACTIVITY

In groups, discuss what the following group names make you think of. Do they suggest anything about what to expect from the music? Dictionaries or a thesaurus could help with this task.

- The Four Tops
- Oasis
- Shampoo
- Metallica
- Take That
- Ultimate Kaos
- Red Hot Chilli Peppers
- Genesis
- Earth, Wind and Fire
- Damned
- Buck's Fizz.

The Young Will Pay The Cost

In the streets of Sarajevo
Life is not that sweet
With people lying around
Even in the Street.

They starve in Ethiopia
For the want of a little food
Donations given kindly
If people are in the mood.

The world knows the story
And everything is lost
But it's the young of the world
Who will pay the cost.

There's kids in the city today
Shooting drugs and popping pills
Snorting cocaine and smoking weed
Knowing that it kills.

There are people in the street tonight
cold and sleeping rough
They have no homes or nice warm beds
God, it must be tough!

The world knows the story
And everything is lost
But it's the young of the world
Who will pay the cost.

So don't be sad, be happy
Just be thankful for
All the things that you have
Who could ask for more.

FIG 3.6 *The image, name and words of a song created by students for a concerned socially aware rap group*

Audience foreknowledge

Very rarely do we come to a star performance without any previous knowledge. Different styles of music demand different expectations about what the performance should be like. For example, heavy metal performances carry the expectation of lights, spectacle and frenetic activity from lead singers, whilst pop music concerts such as those of Take That and other male singing groups carry the expectation of dance routine and energy.

ACTIVITY

As a group, choose a pop group you have not seen in concert and discuss your expectations of their performance.

FIG 3.7 *Pop music tends to make a cult of the virtuoso: the musician whose talents can be spotlighted and admired*

Appearance

Appearance is all important in pop music and image is bound up with the media product itself.

ACTIVITY

Look at Figure 3.7 above and Figure 3.8 on page 54:
- Describe the appearance of the people.
- What kind of music would you associate with these images?

Pop music images carry their own iconography, such as the outfits of stars as diverse as Shirley Bassey or Freddie Mercury.

ACTIVITY

Choose a modern pop group or star you are familiar with. Describe the star/group image and appearance and say how it is linked to the music played.

Part of the image of the star is associated with record/CD covers of both singles and compilations.

ACTIVITY

Bring a selection of covers to the class:
- What connotations do the record/CD sleeves suggest?
- What do the covers contribute to the star/group identity?

Performance

Songs and videos are the expression of the star identity. There are many types of pop videos including:

- stage or studio performance videos
- narrative videos which illustrate the words of the song
- those which draw on genre foreknowledge by setting the song in a horror, western or road-movie type location

- those which are a series of images connected only by the music
- those which use dance particularly to sell the song
- those which are linked to the release of a film and therefore use film clips
- those which use cartoon or animation techniques.

Can you think of any others? Try to give examples for each of the above.

Star resistance

Each song or video that a performer presents adds something to the overall star image, so facets of the star's identity can be highlighted at different times but are rarely completely hidden. When a star in films takes a role which is oppo-

FIG 3.8 *The group and its joint identity is very much part of the pop scene. Working together with co-operation and expertise is part of the myth of the band*

site to his or her usual identity, Dyer calls it star resistance. We can see this with pop stars who become fed up with the same image and want to break out of the rut. This is a business risk but sometimes it can pay off. For example, the singer K. D. Lang started off as a country and western singer but changed style with her single *Constant Craving* in 1992, which was more obviously mainstream pop.

Stars then are a big asset to a record company which will want to sign up exclusive contracts with those who show talent and success.

The pop business

The structure of a major music company is very similar to that of other businesses. Ultimately the owners are the shareholders, but a board of directors represents their interests under the chair of the managing director who has overall responsibility for the success or otherwise of the company.

The list below shows the departments in a typical major company. This is by no means a complete list, but it will give you a flavour of the many jobs involved in record marketing. Discuss in groups what you think the departments are actually concerned with and what problems might arise.

1 **Legal department**
   Contracts
   Copyright
2 **Business affairs**
   Contract negotiation
   Financial budgets
   Music union clearances
3 **Sales and promotion**
   Market research
   Strike force
   TV promo
   Radio pluggers
   Regional radio pluggers
4 **Press department**
   Press officers

5 **Artists and repertoire department**
   Managers
   Talent scouts
   Co-ordinators
6 **Video department**
7 **Travel and transport**
8 **Art department**
9 **Compilations department**
10 **Corporate personal relations** (PR)

ACTIVITY

PROMOTING POP: A SIMULATION
Split into groups of three. Imagine that you work for a record label (either major or indie). You receive the following memos: read and respond to them.

Memo 1
It really is not good enough! We can't blame the shambles of our recent releases on new members of staff. In order to avoid any more disasters like the signing of that German group Bezerk, let us remember a few basic facts. The pop industry is a volatile one. Even successful records have only a short shelf-life (60–180 days) and public taste changes very rapidly. We want the records we release to be successes. We want artists with a clear identity whom we can market competitively. Please look at the latest pop chart. Examine this and then come up with the words for a new song and the name of a group who are going to sing it. Once this task is completed, please write a return memo justifying your decisions.

Memo 2

Now you have written the hit, I expect you to be working for success. In case those of you who have had little success lately have forgotten, company policy is outlined below. You will need:

- profiles of the group, with photographs which could be used for publicity for fan clubs or magazines such as *Just 17*
- an image for the group: clothes, appearance, attitude, etc.
- a news release for the press
- a record/CD cover (montage, drawing or computer generated)
- T-shirt, badges – concept designs
- a list of suitable television appearances
- a storyboard for video
- suggested publicity stunts.

Memo 3

You are doing well! Now carry out these final tasks:

- Record a radio interview with the group.
- Try to persuade DJs to play the song; we do not use payola for radio plugs, so how will you do it?
- Design shop displays and posters.
- Write to our usual people to buy from shops where charts are sampled.

What you have learnt

1 Pop music is a big business which makes a lot of money, not only for artists but also for huge companies.

2 Stars are created and constructed for the media and by the media.

3 Star images are maintained and developed through song releases and increasingly by pop videos.

4 Pop music organisations are huge conglomerates which have many workers at lots of different levels contributing to the success of a particular star.

A question of sport

The media coverage of sport is enormous: on radio, on television, in newspapers and magazines. Sports stars make the front pages nearly as often as other kinds of stars. Most of us spend a good deal of our time not just playing sports but also following sport in the media. Probably the most used medium to follow sport is television, and television organisations like the BBC, ITV and BSkyB compete for the television audience very fiercely.

Until ITV arrived in 1955, the BBC had a monopoly of the major British sporting occasions: the University Boat Race, the Grand National, the Cup Final, the Derby, international rugby matches, Wimbledon, test matches, soccer internationals. In the early days of television, sport was one of the ways in which we created a national identity.

ACTIVITY

Carry out some extended interviews with adults who were growing up in the 1950s. Explore their memories of great sporting occasions on television.

Nowadays the amount and significance of sport in television output has dramatically increased. There is more sport on television because the ratings for sport are so high, and sport increasingly dominates the schedules of the television organisations. Television coverage also affects the timing and organisation of sports events.

ACTIVITY

In this activity you will be using a media research technique called **content analysis**. This technique is used when you need to know how often, how much, when and where a particular kind of content is occurring.

❶ Brainstorm a list of sports as a class.
❷ Break into pairs. Using listings magazines from three consecutive weeks:
  (a) calculate the total number of hours devoted to a single sport
  (b) calculate the total numbers of hours given to live coverage, to recorded highlights, and to other forms of coverage.

❸ Share your results from your sport with the rest of the class.
You should be able to come to some conclusions about:
  ● the total amount of sport in the selected period
  ● the most popular sports covered
  ● the timing of television coverage.
Content analysis can also be used to calculate the importance that different organisations give to sports coverage by working out where in the schedules the sports coverage occurs and whether live sport affects the schedule of an organisation.

Can you think of any drawbacks with this approach to research?

The battle for the audience

Television organisations compete most strongly for live coverage of major sporting events. This is because most live sport attracts large audiences to which the advertisers want access. In 1992 BSkyB Television screened the cricket World Cup from Australia and the sale of dishes went up, which meant that more people were watching. The purpose of a commercial television organisation such as BSkyB is to make a profit for its owners. To pay for the costs of the coverage, BSkyB sells advertising space. The greater the audience, the more advertising; the greater the profits, the more BSkyB can offer for live coverage. BSkyB has been so competitive that Parliament has debated the need to protect the viewer from having to subscribe to BSkyB to see major sporting events.

In the past the BBC covered most of the major sporting events. The BBC can only increase its revenue by increasing the licence fee. Do you think it should be allowed to continue this tradition or should it compete with the commercial organisations?

Quality of coverage

Television organisations not only compete with each other by trying to put in the highest bid for coverage, but they also compete in terms of the quality of coverage.

Presenters

These are the first visible link between the audience and the event. Their job, in co-ordination with the studio, is to orchestrate the whole live presentation. They are not usually linked to one sport and are important in establishing a link between the different sports and the audiences the organisation wants to attract. Media organisations compete for the best presenters.

Commentators

Commentating on a live sports event is a very skilled task. Different sports require different skills. Cricket has lots of gaps which need to be filled by talk; events in rugby happen very quickly.

Experts and analysts

These are famous ex-sportspeople who aim to provide additional information and offer opinions about the performances we witness. They have a role before, during and after the event. They are sometimes in the studio or present at the live event or may even be linked to both of these via satellite. Producers are always looking at new ways of providing expert response for the audience.

Reporters and interviewers

Essentially these have the same functions as people who gather other kinds of news. Look back at Chapter 2 for more information on this subject.

© *MEW*

FIG 3.9 *Catching the moment*

ACTIVITY

Study some of the different kinds of interviews: in the tunnel at half-time, before the event, etc. For each one, work out the purpose of the interview.

Visual conventions

The quality of the visual coverage is also a key issue in the competition. Fans often complain about the quality of the camera work by different organisations. The most obvious issue is the ability of the camera operators to catch the sig-nificant action: the cameras must be pointing at the right bit of the action to make sure the viewer misses nothing. Where the cameras are placed then becomes critical.

ACTIVITY

Study some coverage of your favourite sport from the point of view of:
- camera positions: stump, obstacle, aerial, in car, behind the goal
- shot types: close-up, wide angle, high, low, ground level
- cutting between shots: the way the point of view is controlled
- technical issues: replays.

© MEW

FIG 3.10 *Catching the interview*

Sound

It is interesting to explore the uses of sound. In theory sound adds to the authenticity of the event, but it may sometimes have the opposite effect.

In pairs, explore some of the following issues (choose the topic according to your interest):
- listening to the crowd in a football match
- using a stump microphone in cricket
- listening to referees in any sport who are wired up to a live microphone
- the use of instant replays from a variety of angles
- the use of underwater cameras.

Report your findings to the rest of the class.

Stars and winners

Television organisations search for and focus upon stars and the celebration of victors. Coverage of live events focuses upon the stars in the previews and the post-mortem elements. They are central to the narrative of the live sports event. Here are some typical descriptions used:

- plucked from obscurity
- determined, aggressive, committed, courageous
- model of sportsmanship
- one of us
- classless.

Study your favourite sports star by exploring how television constructs his or her image. Does your star have a rival? Are events in which the two are involved played up as head-to-head confrontations?

MAKING A LIVE BROADCAST

Prepare the coverage of a live sports event in your community. Most of you will not have access to outside broadcast facilities, so break up your planning of the coverage into small segments. Consider the following:

- **Presenter/commentary team/analysts.** You may need auditions, so what are the criteria you will use to choose the best people?
- **Pre-publicity/trailing the coverage.** What will be the focus of your broadcast: key personalities, local rivalries, etc? You will need to pre-plan interviews and plan the running order of the opening section of the programme. What type of publicity will you use: posters, trailing advertisements (TV, radio, newspapers)?
- **Coverage of the event from a technical point of view.** A single camera will mean that live coverage is impossible. Where would be the best camera positions if you had more than one camera and an outside broadcast van with a crew? Would the camera positions be fixed or mobile? Would you use close-ups to dramatise the action? It is here that the frustrations of the technology bite hardest. You can only reflect some of the complexities.

In this essential planning process you will begin to explore some of the issues in and challenges of outside broadcasting. It is not as easy as it is made to look on television!

What you have learnt

1 *Although live sport on television looks and feels real, it is in fact carefully constructed.*

2 *The way it is constructed depends on the particular television organisation. You might like to think further about the placement of advertisements in different sports.*

3 *Television organisations compete fiercely for the highest ratings for their shows and are prepared to disrupt their schedules to cover live sport because it attracts such a high proportion of the available audience. This allows television organisations to attract advertising revenue in the case of commercial organisations, and to justify the licence fee in the case of the BBC.*

4 *Television organisations compete for the audience not only on the basis of cost but also on the quality of their coverage.*

Further thoughts

The three units in this chapter are concerned with the relationship between the audience and the media organisation. You have already explored the ways in which radio organisations seek to brand themselves in the same way as any product, like soap powder or coffee, by organising their whole image and output in relation to the target audience they seek to attract. Popular music and sport are two key areas for the age group 14–24 and you are likely to be involved in one or both of these media products.

The essential thing to grasp is that media organisations cannot exist without an audience and that they compete in a variety of ways for bigger shares of the available audience. This is not only true of the mass media but also of independent and alternative media, though in different ways. Much of the rest of this book is concerned with this complex relationship: the media industries are big business organisations geared to making profits for their owners. It is clear that in this business there are spectacular successes and equally spectacular failures. There are bitter rivalries and acrimonious disputes. There are price wars, cut-throat competitions and claims that the latest media technologies will revolutionise our lives. Things, it is claimed, are getting better and better.

Change seems to be a constant feature of the media:

- new pop groups, styles, stars and dress codes
- new technologies
- more and more apparent choice of media products.

And yet the patterns are often repeated over and over again as media organisations seek to build on the expectations of their audiences. New variants emerge which are linked to their predecessors by patterns of similarity and difference.

Key questions begin to emerge from this relationship:

1 How can the media audience continue to grow?
2 How small an audience do you need to be commercially successful?
3 Who has the power to control what we experience in the media?
4 Are we controlled by media representations?
5 Can we control the media?
6 Are we passive consumers of commercial commodities manipulated by commercial interests?
7 Will media producers trivialise media

productions in order to appeal to the largest audience? Will the schedules be dominated by entertainment?

You will need to keep coming back to questions like these and there are no easy answers. This and the remaining chapters of the first part of this book raise these and other questions in a variety of ways through case studies. Case studies are another important way of working when you are a media student. You can study one aspect of an issue, such as an aspect of the relationship between audiences and organisations, in a detailed way using a variety of approaches (research, practical work, interviewing, etc.) and link what you find out to wider issues. In this way you can build up your knowledge, skills and understanding gradually until you become an expert if you want to. As a media student you may want to specialise later in your favourite medium: most people do. In fact many people working in the media industries do so because they became fascinated by some aspect of media production as a consumer and want to make their own contribution. Case studies also give the examples which you need when you are presenting your opinions and points of view on media issues.

4

Media issues

Batman: the case of the Caped Crusader

Batman has been one of the most popular fictional characters ever invented. He has appeared in all sorts of media texts since the first comic strip in May 1939.

- Which ones can you remember?
- What was Batman like?
- Can you draw him?

This section is about Batman and his relationship with his audience. How has he managed to remain so popular? Is Batman today what he was 30 years ago? How will Batman have to change in the future? Will Batman survive? Will Batman ever grow old and die? The saga continues.

Holy futures!

A C T I V I T Y

THE BAT FACTS TRIVIA QUIZ
❶ Hum the theme tune to the 1960s television series.
❷ Which character in the film *Batman* has got green hair and white skin and a grotesque grin? A bonus mark if you can name the actor who played the character.
❸ Who is Batman's assistant?
❹ Did Batgirl first appear in the television series or the comic?

❺ In which city does Batman have his adventures?
❻ Who in *Batman Returns* says to Batman, 'You're just jealous because I'm a genuine freak and you have to wear a mask'?
❼ Has Batgirl ever appeared in a film?
❽ Which pop singer's songs are featured in the film *Batman*?
❾ In the animated TV series, which actor has the voice-over for The Joker: Tommy Lee Jones, Madonna or Mark Hamill? A bonus mark if you can name another film that this actor starred in.
❿ Who plays Catwoman in *Batman Returns*? A bonus mark if you spell the name correctly.

The fans

Now look at the answers on page 64. If you scored more than ten points you are a fan! Fans are nearly always experts on their chosen character, series, group, sports team, star and so on. Are you a fan of anything or anyone? Many people think that to be a fan means that you follow your chosen media product in a mindless way and that eventually you will grow out of your obsession. There is some element of truth in this. Fans can sometimes become obsessive and see things only from a single viewpoint.

Answers: Trivia quiz
2. The Joker/Jack Nicholson
3. Robin
4. TV
5. Gotham City
6. The Penguin
7. No
8. Prince
9. Mark Hamill/Star Wars Trilogy
10. Michelle Pfeiffer

However, fans are also a very important audience category for media organisations as they feed back messages to the producers about their product. Fans will earnestly discuss not only the latest goings on in their chosen media product, but also a range of very complicated technical, presentational and narrative conventions. Soap opera fans, for example, are especially good at spotting inconsistencies in the presentation of characters or storylines; they can have phenomenal memories.

The letters pages of specialist magazines and comics are an important convention which controls the feed back responses from the readers about the issues which concern them. These letters can be very passionately one-sided, but are very often extremely well informed. Often they are the most read section of the magazine, as the readers can feel part of a community committed to the past, present and future of the media product.

ACTIVITY

Study Figure 4.1 on pages 66–7, which shows letters from Batman comic fans about one of the stories printed in 1967.

- List the different issues the fans bring up about the story.
- How old do you think the writers are?
- What is the editor trying to do in the replies to the letters (another letters page convention).

The front cover

The covers of comics and magazines are closely connected to the kinds of audience that they hope to attract. A cover must be distinctive and eye-catching so that it is picked up and purchased. As one of the fans points out in his letter, it is important that the front cover is of high quality.

ACTIVITY

Study Figure 4.2 on page 68. How is the front cover organised to persuade an audience to pick it up and buy it?

A front cover is also a trailer for the contents. Identify two elements of the front page which try to persuade the reader to look at the rest of the comic.

The central characters

The appearance and behaviour of the central characters is probably the area attracting most comment from fans. Studying representations of the central characters from different time periods and different media is an important way of understanding how they are re-represented. The similarities are as important as the differences.

Look at the Batman video covers shown in Figure 4.3 on page 69. Study the representations of the central characters by comparing the screen shots of the animated version to the other representations. Which of the others is it most like? From which is it most different?

Study Figure 4.4 on pages 70–1, an interview with Kevin Conroy who is the voice of Batman in the animated version. What issues does he bring out about Batman? Do you agree with him?

What is the audience classification for each of these Batman films?

❶ *Batman* (1989)   PG/12/15/18
❷ *Batman Returns* (1992)   PG/12/15/18
❸ *Batman Forever* (1995)   PG/12/15/18

Your answers to this activity will tell you something about the ways in which the stories have been presented. It has always been important how Batman behaves. It is very common to regard him as an example of a superior being, a superhero. However, the emphasis from the beginning has been on him as a man. He has never had superpowers. He succeeds through ingenuity, skill and integrity as he faces everything the criminal world can throw at him. He survives by wit, daring, ingenuity and technology. Famously, in *Batman 47*, he declares:

❝ *Criminals are a superstitious, cowardly lot, so I must wear a disguise that will strike terror into their hearts! I must be a creature of the night, like a . . . a . . . a bat!* ❞

He is a man dressed as a bat who seeks revenge on the criminal community who murdered his parents in cold blood in front of him when he was a child. Batman has, therefore, always been a favourite character in terms of distinguishing between right and wrong. This was a popular theme in the 1950s in America.

Do the films change our view of Batman?

The stories

Look at Figure 4.2 again. It has 'Approved by The Comics Code Authority' in the top right-hand corner with a unique logo. This was a voluntary code in which the publishers of comics in the 1950s agreed amongst themselves about representation in comics. Although still in existence today, many publishers do not take much notice of it. The code banned violence, explicit sex, violence for violence's sake and the triumph of evil or anti-social behaviour. In particular, it said that the upholders of law and order should never be represented in a bad light.

Read the story *Secret of the Slaying Statues* printed in Figure 4.5 on pages 72–6. You may find it interesting to act out the story by using the speech balloons and the captions (the bits where the writer talks to the reader).

❶ What is the crime in the story? Briefly explain how Batman overcomes the criminal to solve the mystery?
❷ Who or what helps him to do this? Are all of these convincing? Some of the fans often comment on the unconvincing bits of the stories.
❸ How does Batman speak to the good characters? Make a list of the way he identifies them. How does he address the baddies? How does this fit in with The Comics Code? Do you feel that the story is dated?
❹ One of the fans says in his letter (Figure 4.1) that 'The story started out well, with the right amounts of action and intellect. Batman's . . . deductions were very good, fitting right into the detective groove you are molding him for . . .' Do these comments apply to this story?
❺ The same fan goes on to add '. . . it is important to picture him, not as an infallible robot, but as a human who *can* make mistakes . . .' Does Batman make any mistakes in this story?

The illustrators

Fans of the comics are influenced not only by the stories themselves, but also by the way in which different illustrators/artists draw them. They have a clear sense of what they feel is of high quality and what styles are suitable for different stories. Adaptors of the Batman story

Dear Editor:

"The Mystery of Frank Robbins", I feel, would make an interesting case for *The Batman* himself. Half the time Frank will write a real bomb and then he'll write a real gem like his current story, "Challenge of the Consumer Crusader," in *Detective* #415. What made it so great? This:

(1) Frank's not-so-subtle take-off on *Ralph Nader and his Raiders*.

(2) *The Batman* disguised as Carson's ghost.

(3) The way *Batguy* escaped death from the car. Superb!

There's a lot more, but I'm not going in to knit-picking. One thing, though, is the beautiful Brown-Giordano art. Kinda makes me remember Brown's old days on the *Challs* (sniff).

I must say that I can hardly wait for Frank Robbins' comix magazine art. He's a fine artist and I hope his work is as all-around as it is in his *Johnny Hazard* syndicate strip.

—*JOE FARARA, Canton, Mass.*

(Frank Robbins' Man-Bat art in #416 will be reader-evaluated in next issue's HOT-LINE. Also forthcoming in this issue is another Robbins' script-art double-header. "Forecast for Tonight—Murder!" Meanwhile, there's a Robbins-roast coming up in the next letter!—JS)

*****

Dear Editor:

Julius Schwartz, you should be ashamed of yourself! When the reprint stories are so much better than the new stories that they make the new stories seem silly (I take that back—they didn't seem silly . . . they WERE silly!), something is wrong! The best thing about *Tec 415* was the cover, which was good, except that it was so crammed with blurbs you could hardly make out the drawing.

But enough chatter; on to the heart of the matter. . . . First, we attack the lead story, featuring *Batman*, by custom, "Challenge of the Consumer Crusader". . . . Aha, Ha, ha, Ha, ha! You've *got* to be kidding, Julie, baby! People don't get hit by refrigerator doors in fights or dropped from cars even in *Sugar and Spike!* Not to mention the typical baldie millionaires giving in to pressure. *Yicchh!* If I want a satire, I'll ask for it. Frank Robbins is a pretty good writer when he wants to be, but when he is in a so-so mood, disaster is usually inevitable.

Yes, the mind is staggered by what this man can do! In one issue he can make a complete mockery out of the great *Batman* we have known—the dark, dreaded avenger of the thirties, the great detective and champion of justice of the forties, the costumed hero (!?) of the fifties (WELL, that's what he was!), the apple of the science-fiction lover's eyes in the sixties; to this—the complete boob of the Frank Robbins age! What gags me is that he doesn't *have* to do this! Remember "The Gal Most Likely to Marry Batman", "Challenge of the Man-Bat", and "You Die by Mourning"? Hmm? Oh, the Brown-Giordano art was good, but *BM's* ears on his mask were too narrow.

It looks like I'm really roasting Frank Robbins this letter, but, really, he shouldn't have anything to do with *Batgirl* at all. He just can't, or else doesn't, capture her sort of haughty, cock-sure personality into his too formulated stories. They would be all right in a *Gangbusters*-type strip, starring any old police man or woman; but *Batgirl* isn't just some ol' police man (!) or woman; she's *Batgirl*, not the rather flimsy character Robbins portrays her as. He's really not suited to a detective-type story. Don Heck's art helped "Death Shares the Spotlight" immensely, but his rough drawings are more suited to the war mags than *Batgirl*.

What're you mad at me for?! I told ya I liked the cover and reprints!

—*KEITH GRIFFIN, Mobile, Ala.*

*****

Dear Editor:

There are many fans who read comix today, who labor under the illusion that Denny O'Neil and Neal Adams are the only people in the world who can, respectively, write and draw *The Batman*. This assumption is, of course, patently ridiculous—and Frank Robbins, Bob Brown, and Dick Giordano proved the above statement with "Challenge of the Consumer Crusader!"

The story started out well, with the right amounts of action and intellect. *Batman's* in-flight deductions were very good, fitting right into the detective groove you are molding him for. The clue of the polished shoes was, by the way, a good example of the way all *Batman* deductions should be. Hinging on some little fact that the reader can see if he looks hard enough. I also enjoyed the brief scene where the *Caped Logician* was rescued by Tom Carson. *The Batman* can take care of himself, but it is important to picture him, not as an infallible robot, but as a human who *can* make mistakes.

From a technical viewpoint, this was a good script. By page six we're already deep into the plot, with one murder attempt foiled and one suspect already on the grill. The character of Ben Ames was very realistically portrayed. As a man up against the wall, faced with false accusations, he acted as a real human might to save himself and his business. The phosphorescent ghost-bit was a bit old, but we'll chalk its effectiveness up to Ames' distraught state, okay?

Page nine was a personal shot of *The Batman*. One can almost see the pieces of the puzzle falling into place in his mind as he drives to Carson's testing plant. Up to page nine, the story progressed without a hitch.

Pages ten, eleven and twelve got rather silly, with the test-equipment doing the fighting for *The Batman*. It brought back unwelcome memories of the *Batman*-TV show, wherein *camp* (shudder) gimmicks were the utmost in cuteness. Bob Brown's art, however, reminded me of some of his best *Challengers of the Unknown* days.

Batman again became a human being on page thirteen. He, the man with the computer brain, was, indeed, *suckered* into a trap. A very original, but logical trap, I might add. But why couldn't *The Batman* simply have used his rope and swung out a window to safety?

Anyway, a very good story, altogether. Which is

FIG 4.1 *Letters from Batman fans*

more than I can say for "Death Shares the Spotlight!" The story was just about all action, which made for little intellectual enjoyment.

In the reprint section, I thoroughly enjoyed *Mysto*. The plot was inspired. More *Mysto* reprints, please.

"The Case of the Finders Keepers" was a good story, but became a bit gimmicky at the end with the cyclotron and all. But there's nothing you can do about that.

So far, *Detective Comics* has been worth 25¢. I hope for expanded-length stories in the future. Will my hopes be realized?
—MIKE W. BARR, Akron, Ohio

(As you have and will observe, the new material is being expanded a page or so at a time. What the ratio will eventually be between new-and-reprint material is something only you, the cash customer, can resolve.—JS)

*****

Dear Editor:
Writing for a long-range medium—in this case comix, where five months can pass between scripting and publication—and trying to keep up with the trends at the same time is an exacting science. Most comix writers aren't very good scientists, to say the least; witness the continued use of phrases like "Right On" (that's groovy, man—or at least it was two years ago). But Frank Robbins has been very lucky this time around in plotting his latest script around Consumer Advocate Ralph Nader and his *Raiders* (or, if you'd rather, "Tom Carson and his Consumer Commandos"). With the mass media still in heated controversy over the man, you've jumped onto the bandwagon just in time.

With topicality as a springboard, "Challenge of the Consumer Crusader" fared very well. It didn't reveal anything about car companies using chewing gum for weldings, or the Bon Vivant Soup Company dumping germs in leek soup—neither of which Robbins could've pulled through with any success, judging from his other attempts at social relevance—but instead used topicality as a vehicle for an otherwise implausible story. There had to be a *reason* for all that action, including hydraulic lifts trying to pulverize *The Batman* and giant cranes dumping him in a car onto a concrete floor—and Tom Carson's Testing Plant was a nice excuse, although a little reminiscent of the Bill Finger era in which *Batman* would be forever chasing crooks up huge soda fountain exhibits, climbing up gigantic model movie projectors, and thirty-foot-tall moving statues of Don Quixote.

Aside from the final climactic action sequence—which took up far more of the story than it should've—the story, although not a whodunit, was clever. Frank Robbins exploited to the fullest his expert ability as an "Onion Peeler"—with each successive revelation and clue, the story became more absorbing and puzzling. It's unfortunate that this only lasted the first ten pages of the story. The remaining five pages of action became tiring and then totally implausible.
—CLEM ROBINS, Sheffield, Mass.

(Is "action" still the name of this game, or—as the previous correspondent complained, "the story was just about all action, which made for little intellectual enjoyment"? Is there an acceptable ratio between the two?—JS)

*****

Dear Editor:
Sometimes simplicity IS the best! Without any actual story-telling gimmicks or spectacular characters, Frank Robbins created a fascinating tale in "Challenge of the Consumer Crusader." The mystery element was present in large doses and *Batman* was effectively utilized. Even Bob Brown put a little extra into the artwork, which seemed to be influenced by Neal Adams. The ears of *Batman's* cowl were lengthened and the cape was a bit more flowing. Not to forget Dick Giordano, who does more for Mr. Brown than any other inker in breathing life and excitement into the art.

The *Batgirl* tale showed promise last issue, but fell apart this ish. There is a suggestion I'd like to make. As you may know, *Lois Lane* #114 carries a novel-length tale combining *Lois* and *The Thorn*, the back-up feature of that mag. Well, why not run a 22-page tale in Detective co-starring *Batman* and *Batgirl?* I believe that a full-lengther would be a first for this mag. Also, we haven't seen *Batman* and *Batgirl* team up for quite a while. So how about it?
—GERARD TRIANO, Elmont, N.Y.

(Frank Robbins has been mulling over a team-up adventure of Batman *and* Batgirl. *Soon as it jells,* Man *will meet Girl!—JS)*

*****

Dear Editor:
When I first look into a new issue of *Detective*, I search for two things: Did Neal Adams draw *The Batman* and have they taken Don Heck off *Batgirl*. Since both questions were answered negatively in #415, I sat down to enjoy a good, but not great, issue.

"Challenge of the Consumer Crusader" was interesting, but flawed. First, the good points. It had a unique twist on the old extortion racket plot and *The Batman* was given a good deathtrap to escape from—the falling car. Seeing Babs Gordon in curlers was a beautiful touch. (What would happen if she suddenly was needed as *Batgirl?*) Would she have to fix her hair? Hmmm?!) Now for the flaws. This story lacked the ingredients of a "classic" detective story because no clues or suggestions were given ahead of time. *Batman* suddenly stumbled onto the villains. Secondly, the fight scene. The torture-test machines attacking the gang was a bit too much. However, with Bob Brown's art, the good points outweighed the bad.

Now to *Batgirl*. Considering the space available, the plot was okay, but I believe Don Heck's art is completely wrong for this strip. Try giving her a story where she is more like *The Batman*, swooping from the shadows to strike fear into . . . you know what!
—BILL FOX, Scottdale, Pa.

*****

Dear Editor:
The early stories which marked the return of *The Batman* had Bruce Wayne getting involved with people via his *Victims, Incorporated* organization. However, since then, we have seen nary a trace of this. Could it be that Bruce has decided to let *Batman* do all the work as he goes back to being a playboy?

"Challenge of the Consumer Crusader" seems to support this point. *Batman* is the one doing all the helping out in the story. Bruce Wayne is not to be seen.

How about bringing back that "new" side of *Batman's* alter ego that we saw for a brief moment?
—BOB ROZAKIS, Elmont, N.Y.

(Another problem in ratios: How much of the story action should be divided up between Bruce Wayne *and* The Batman?—JS)

*****

Address communications to BATMAN'S HOT-LINE, National Periodical Publications, 909 Third Ave., New York, N.Y. 10022.

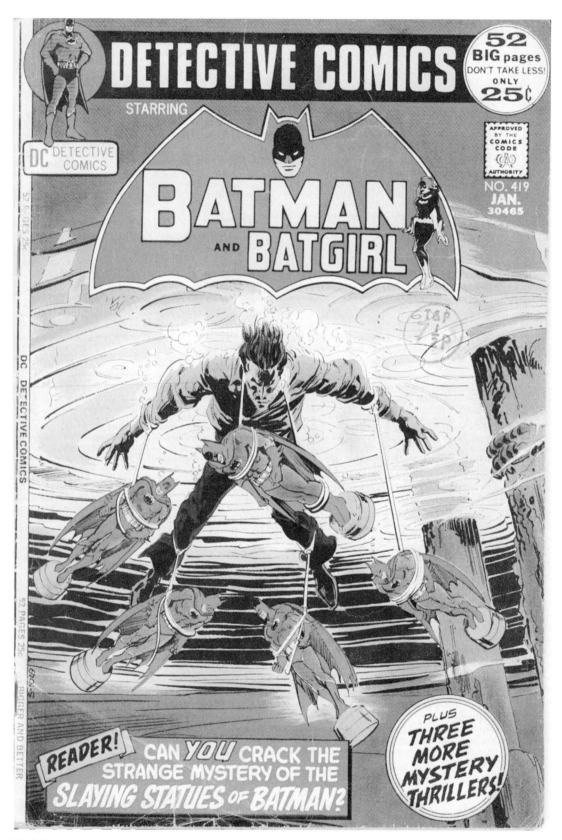

FIG 4.2

FIG 4.3 *Batman video covers*

VIEWS FROM THE BATCAVE

Kevin Conroy — Batman Animated

WERE you a Batman fan as a child?

I was of the television series. That was more my generation. It was fun, but I don't know if it would stand up to today's TV standards because it was so campy. But for the Sixties it was great.

It's totally different from your animated show which is taken very seriously.

It is. It is done so beautifully. It goes back to the original style, and is very dark and very *film noir*-ish and Deco in its style, and that's much more the Dark Knight. Mark Hamill [voice of The Joker] and I did most of the early shows together. We'd been recording episodes every week and didn't really have anything to grab onto visually. They had shown us sketches of things but we didn't have any real animation to look at. We went into loop the first shows that came back from the animators a good six months after we recorded them. We both were shocked seeing what they had produced on a big screen, the quality and the colours and the graphics and the musical score, a full symphony that was so lush, I remember the moment, we were both just so shocked.

How did you get the job doing the series?

It was really just a general acting audition. They put out a call for people to submit voice tapes. What they were specifically looking for were actors who do more stage and film work than actors who do more exclusively voice work. They wanted more of an actor sound than a commercial sound. I just did a tape of about five or six different characters, and they immediately called me in. They had hundreds of people for each character. They were deluged because everyone wanted to be involved. It was very competitive, and I just got called in within a couple of weeks to meet the producers.

When they called you in did they show you any drawings of what their concept of Batman would be?

Yes, they had elemental sketches. The thing that they kept saying over and over again was, 'just use your imagination, think Dark Knight. That's the image we're going for.' So my voice got deeper and huskier and more breathy. It got very whispered and very deep and they loved that, it was exactly the sound, that sort of smokey dark sound. It is hard to maintain, because you're crunching down on your vocal cords, but he's not a man of many words!

What about Bruce Wayne? Did you adjust your voice in any way to do that?

Yeah, to get a nice dramatic change originally I was doing his voice even higher than mine, sort of a Connecticut locked-jaw quality to dramatize the difference. But the first three or four episodes came back from the animators and he sounded too élitist, too snobby. So I redid all those episodes with a voice closer to mine. The distinction was fine because I was going so deep for the Batman voice that I didn't really have to do that much different than my own voice for Bruce Wayne.

Tell a little about the process of mak-

ing an animated series.

What fascinated me when I first started, because I'd never done an animated voice before, was that we [the actors] are first, I had no idea. I thought we would be looping artwork that had been in process for months, but the voices are first. We are in a sound studio and each person has his own little cubicle and there may be, depending on the size of the cast for that episode, seven or nine people in that room. Each one of you has your own microphone and headsets and you do it like an old fashioned radio play. We all have full scripts and we act it out. What fascinated me is that we were the first

FIG 4.4 *An interview with Kevin Conroy, the voice of Batman in the animated version*

The CCCs — Cartoon Caped Crusaders

"They wanted to go back to the original concept" says Conroy of the animated Batman

step of the creative process, so we got to really influence the script a lot and that influences the animation. The writers, director and producers are there for every episode so the booth is full of the entire creative team of the show. So if you get line idea changes they're right there. We do one episode a week.

I've read articles on animated films where actors do a character and never meet anyone else in the movie. Is it unusual that you all work together?
It's fantastic because we really do interact as the other person's performance affects you. Sometimes it happens that we can't if there's a star that is going to do a certain voice, who's doing a movie somewhere. They may come in and just loop their voice, but for the most part everyone's there.

When I saw the show I thought the animation reflected the comics. Did

they try and emulate the comics?
That's exactly what they wanted to do, to go back to the original comic book and they did not draw off anything from the Sixties' TV show or any of the more recent comic books. They wanted to go back to the original concept which is why this thing took off so high.

Robin wasn't in the movie, Batman: Mask of the Phantasm...
At that point he still wasn't in many episodes. If we do a second movie they've told us he will be in it. There has been a lot of talk since Christmas about doing a major theatrical release movie, because **Phantasm** was originally written and designed to be a video release movie. Once they got it back from the first cut they realized that they had a feature on their hands, and why send it straight to video? But they never really completely got behind it as a theatrical release. They

didn't spend the distribution money that would have been necessary, because it had never been budgeted for it. You can't just suddenly invent a few million dollars, so they decided to release it theatrically and see how it did and, considering they spent no money at all distributing it, it did very respectably. There was a big audience out there that was interested in seeing it.

What are the advantages of doing Batman as an animated feature?
You're relying on the audience's imagination a lot more with animation, and you're creating a world of surreal reality. You can do anything with time and space and structure. Anything can happen with animation. People can change before your eyes. With live action it's all very tangible and hard, there's a real hard reality to it, there's only so much you can do.

If you do another movie what direction would you like to see it go?
I think the closer it stays to its roots the better it is. The familiar villains become as much old friends as the heroes. Sometimes when they introduce a new more bizarre villain I find the line kind of odd.

What do you think of Tim Burton's concept of Batman?
They were beautifully made, they were very well acted, they were lavishly shot, but I had one small criticism that really bugged me, and that was not just the level of violence, but the kind of violence. In *Batman: The Animated Series*, no one ever dies and children are never in danger. There are certain lines that don't get crossed. In the Tim Burton movie when the Ice Princess crashed through the glass ceiling and plunged to her death I gasped, and the place was as silent as a grave. Some parents left with their kids, and I thought 'It's not even fun anymore'. From then on you were scared. I just thought that he, in pursuing his dark, dark view of that world, went too dark and he crossed the line with kids.

Why do you think the phenomena has kept growing and growing?
I think that's the sign of a real quality endeavour. I think any kind of performing art or creative art that has integrity, and is really based in quality, doesn't dissipate over time but gets richer and attracts more of an audience. This is a really high quality animated piece. It's only going to get richer. This is the kind of character that can really transcend generations and last a long, long time. And yet, when you look at it objectively, it's a grown man running around in tights and a Batman cape! There's something ridiculous to it!

Judy Sloane

FIG 4.5

9

I... DON'T GET IT--! YOU WAS KNOCKED OUT!

Y-YOU'RE G-GONNA ASK ME TO T-TALK... AND I W-WILL

WE'RE SEAMEN OFF THE FREIGHTER "LUCY B," DOWN TO PIER 17!

WHO'S YOUR BOSS?

DREAM ON, FELLA! I KNEW THE HEAD-BLOW WAS COMING...

...SO I RODE WITH IT--AND FAKED UNCONCIOUSNESS!

WE DO A BIT O' FREE-LANCE SMUGGLING ON THE SIDE...TONIGHT WE'RE SUPPOSED TO PICK UP A SHIPMENT OF GOLD!

HIS NAME IS...AGGH!

ZING!

10

HE'S BEEN SHOT...DEAD!-- BY SOMEONE WITH A HIGH-POWERED RIFLE!

THE KILLER WAS PROBABLY AFRAID TO GO FOR ME! OR MAYBE HE MISSED...?

THE SHOT COULD HAVE COME FROM ANY ONE OF THOSE SHADOWS...OR ALLEYS!

I'VE GOT TO DOPE OUT A TRAP...

OVER IN KILLARNEY, MINNY YEARSH AGO...

ME MITHER SANG A SONG FER...

EH? TH' BATMAN! I DIDN'T MEAN TO BE SINGIN' LOUD, SOR!

I'M NOT SCOLDING YOU, CHUM-- I HAVE A JOB FOR YOU!

IT HAPPENS SWIFTLY...THE CAPED CRUSADER PHONES COMMISSIONER GORDON...

TELEPHONE

...AND WITHIN MINUTES, A PLATOON OF GRIM, BLUE-CLAD OFFICERS CONVERGES ON AN ANCIENT SHIP, SERVICE-REVOLVERS DRAWN...

LUCY B

THERE IS NO RESISTANCE. SWIFTLY, EFFICIENTLY, THE SHIP'S COMPANY IS TAKEN INTO CUSTODY...

11

IN THE CARGO HOLD, THE COMMISSIONER FINDS SEVERAL TONS OF PURE GOLD...

WHILE A FEW BLOCKS AWAY, THE MERRIMENT CONTINUES INTO THE WEE HOURS, THE LAUGHING MOB UTTERLY UNAWARE OF THE DRAMA OCCURRING ON THE DOCKS...

HOT DOGS

SAUSAGES

ONE BLURRY BROTH OF A LADDIE IN PARTICULAR SEEMS TO BE HAVING A GOOD TIME...

...ME HOME IS IN DUBLIN...'TIS WHERE I WAS WEANED...

AH, I WISHT YA COULD'VE SEEN IT! THE BATMAN HIMSELF ASKIN' ME TA GO FER THE PO-LICE...

...AN' TAKIN' ME INTO HIS CONFIDENCE, HE WAS!

TOLD ME HE KNOWS THE RINGLEADER OF THE VILLAINS, INDEED, INDEED...

SAYS HE'LL BE WAITIN' FER THE BADDIE, TA CLUTCH HIM IN A TRAP!

12

SUDDENLY, A LOOK OF PANIC CROSSES A CERTAIN FACE IN THE CROWD...HE BEGINS WALKING, QUICKLY, STIFFLY...

...AWAY FROM THE NOISE AND LIGHTS, HE BREAKS INTO A RUN--

AND STUMBLES TO AN ABRUPT HALT AS A POWERFUL FIGURE LOOMS IN HIS PATH!

PERHAPS HE SENSES HIS PLIGHT AS HOPELESS AS HE CLUTCHES AT HIS WEAPON...

...PERHAPS!

17

colour-washed the frames, so as you're turning the pages there will be four or five frames totally washed in blue and the next page they're all washed in red ... So we kept the sense of the city, but it's always washed in a very dense colour. **9**

So she is adapting a comic book tradition for the new medium of film. She is also adding to the tradition. Gotham City is also seen for the first time from the air via helicopter shots of two real American cities, New York and Los Angeles, to create the authentic feel of the city. All the previous films had used studio sets.

The props and gadgets

This has always been a controversial area for fans. Every time Batman has been adapted for film and television there have been more variations. How many gadgets can you remember that Batman uses? Did you remember them all from the films, the TV series, the comics or somewhere else?

(comic, film, animation) want to draw on its traditions and add something of their own to the saga: they want a special place in the history of the famous legend. Lots of the illustrators were comic fans before they were illustrators.

ACTIVITY

Have you any new ideas for Bat gadgets? Imagine a situation which looks impossible for Batman/Batwoman to get out of and then invent a gadget that will help them. Do you think Bat fans will approve of your gadget?

The setting

Batman has always been set in the city. The production designer on the film *Batman Forever* was Barbara Ling. Traditionally, because of the bat being a creature of the night, this has often meant dark tones. This film is different. Barbara, in an interview for the *Batman Souvenir Special*, tells us:

6 *The thing I loved about the comics, especially the* Dark Night *series, is that they*

The villains

The villain in recent years has been attracting as much, if not more, attention as Batman himself. Why do you think this is? Think about the villains in the films: The Joker, The Riddler, Catwoman. In what ways are the villains similar to each other and in what ways are they different?

Here is a list of villains from the comics who have not yet appeared in any screen versions of *Batman*: The Bookworm, Egghead, Fingers, The Black Widow, Mr Freeze.

Choose one, then write a character profile by answering the following questions:
- In what way is the character evil?
- What are his or her particular skills and abilities?
- Does he or she have special powers?
- How does he or she speak?
- How does he or she dress?
- What links does he or she have with other villains?
- Where does he or she come from?

If you are good at drawing, draw your chosen character in a typical pose.

Storyboard a short film sequence in which your chosen villain confronts Batman/Batwoman for the first time.

What you have learnt

❶ *Fans are a very important audience category because they know so much about the history of a particular genre, star or programme. Many media producers who choose particular projects do so because they themselves are fans.*

❷ *Media producers need to repeat the traditions whilst at the same time adding something original to attract new audiences.*

❸ *By comparing versions of a text like* Batman, *you can learn something about history and attitudes to social issues such as crime, young people and urban violence through the media representations.*

Looking into computer games

Some people claim that computer games are bad for you. They say that young children and teenagers who use computer games become isolated, anti-social and even sometimes addicted to playing games. This unit asks you to explore these kinds of criticisms by finding out what uses young children make of computer games and what pleasures such games give them.

© MEW   © MEW

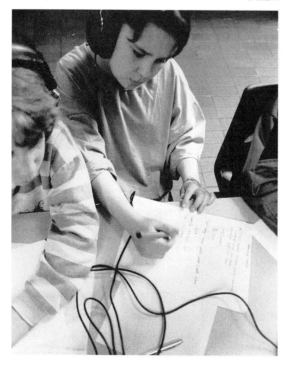

© MEW

FIG 4.6 *Some alternative views of young consumers*

The second half of the unit asks you to describe and analyse some of the ways in which computer games are marketed and audiences are built up into mass audiences. This is a very important issue in media studies because of the very popular idea that people, especially young people, are passive victims of the media and that they are being manipulated by the companies who produce these games through their marketing techniques.

The effects of the media

At one time or another most of the media forms have been questioned in terms of their effects on people. You've probably heard a few of the following criticisms:

- Pop music makes you deaf.
- Reading comics is bad for your reading.
- Too much television makes you into a couch potato.
- Watching violent videos makes you violent.
- Power Rangers make you want to imitate them.
- Cartoons encourage bad and violent behaviour.

It is easy to make fun of such ideas, but there are other viewpoints about the effects of the media:

1 Comics have very important roles in educating young people about the environment (e.g. Greenpeace) and drugs (e.g. in many of our cities).
2 Soap opera characters who have faced really difficult problems are often quoted as being important as role models (e.g. Mark Fowler in *EastEnders* or Beth Jordache in *Brookside*). Other characters' reactions to them reflect different viewpoints and can become a focus for change through discussion in playgrounds and pubs.
3 Pop stars have often promoted good causes (e.g. Bob Geldof (Live Aid) or Sting (The Amazon Rainforest)) claiming to show that by using the power of the media ordinary people can influence events in the world.
4 Many advertisements seek to improve people's behaviour (e.g. AIDS awareness and drink-driving campaigns).

So it is not easy to make up your mind about the effects of the media. There are a lot of complicated issues involved. Lots of people have opinions on this which they will tell you are right and you will hear contradictory viewpoints.

We suggest you keep an open mind and see what you can find out about the effects of the media using computer games as a case study. Computer games are a good place to start studying effects because you probably know more about them than other age groups and many of the games are clearly aimed at people like you.

ACTIVITY

An important research method in all the media is **focus groups**. These are interviews which are held to find out how a group of people feel about an issue (e.g. violence in children's cartoons), a service (e.g. the programming policy of a local radio station) or a product (e.g. a new computer game). You are going to use a focus group to explore young children's knowledge of, their uses of, and their attitudes towards computer games.

Stage 1: Choosing the group
The group of people you choose will be appropriate to your circumstances, but we suggest that you bear in mind the following points:
- they should be younger than you are
- they must use computer games
- they must be good talkers and listeners.
Gender is an issue in the use of computer games, so do you want a mixed group?

Stage 2: Preparing for the discussion
Draw up a series of prompt questions based on what you need to find out:

- the range of games used by the group
- favourite game(s)
- how much time they spend on games
- how much money they spend on games
- what makes a good game
- what their parents feel about the games
- how they find out about games: friends, a games shop, television
- their knowledge of related comics, magazines and films.

The more time you spend thinking about these questions the better.

Stage 3: Carrying out the discussion

1 You will need a quiet space where you can record the conversation. A single fixed video camera which shows all the faces is one option. Another is the use of a table microphone and an audio-cassette. Another is to have a partner who can record notes of the discussion (choose someone who is a good writer).

2 Introduce yourself to the group and, if necessary, introduce the participants to each other.

3 Before you begin you will need to explain the purpose of the focus group. If you are recording the group, explain that the reason for this is to quote accurately what has been said in your report. Explain that they will only be named if they want to be.

4 Tell them also that all opinions are valuable and that no one is ever wrong in this kind of discussion.

5 Direct questions at an individual in the group rather than to the group in general. Start with simple information/description questions to get things going. Be prepared to move away from your questions if it looks interesting. Don't force the discussion but keep in mind your objectives.

6 Follow up interesting points by asking for more information or comments from other people.

7 Don't allow strong characters to dominate. Leading such groups is not easy, but it is an important skill in all sorts of situations and is therefore worth the effort involved.

Stage 4: Presenting your findings

You may choose to write a report or present your findings to an audience as a media text.

The medium you choose will affect your final presentation. However, the following general points apply:

- Your audience need to know who you are and why you were interested in the issue.
- They need to know the make-up of the focus group and why they were chosen as representative.
- You need to highlight central issues that arose from the discussion.
- You need to describe the insights that your research gave you and any conclusions you came to. You should be careful with these as your focus group was small.

Marketing the games

We are now going to turn our attention to the ways in which the producers of computer games target particular consumer groups and compete with each other to sell more of their products.

There are two main producers of computer console systems in Great Britain: Sony who manufactures the PlayStation games system and Sega who manufactures the Saturn console games system. Both are sophisticated systems offering fighting games, racing games and platform games with high-quality graphics and sound. In 1995 and 1996 these two manufacturers spent £45 million in marketing their products. Each company is aiming to dominate the computer games market. In 1994 people spent £538 million on computer games in Britain. So you can see there is a lot to play for!

One major way in which the companies hope to achieve market domination is through the use of advertising and publicity based on careful market research. Both organisations have developed marketing campaigns.

Marketing campaigns

Marketing campaigns can involve a number of approaches and activities:

1 **Intensive TV advertising.** Can you describe any advertisements for computer games from memory? Cinema advertising is even more important. Why do you think this is? Other possibilities include elaborate marketing stunts or events, air balloons, laser displays, etc. Have you heard of any?
2 **Sponsorship of public events.** Have there been any near you?
3 **Trickle down marketing.** The marketing team tries to make sure that influential people like TV announcers, pop stars, and style leaders such as the footballer Ryan Giggs are associated with its product and so set a trend. Often this is through merchandising objects like T-shirts.
4 **Product placement.** The games are made into a logical part of a soap opera, or a series or a film. They are not advertised directly but are used by one or more of the characters in the drama. Although this is prohibited in British television at present, you might spot the games occasionally as attitudes are changing. Anyway you can have a lot of fun identifying how many brand names appear in your favourite soap or serial. You will find more evidence of this practice in American films. In the USA there are between 15 and 30 companies whose only business is to try to place products into media programmes. Coca-Cola and Pepsi have their own business sections devoted to such activities.
5 **Linking the games to popular characters in cartoon programmes and comics.** It is very likely that you already know some examples of this.
6 **Offering the games as prizes in quiz/game shows.** Organisations give their products free so that they can be seen by a mass audience. There are now examples of game shows which can offer this kind of embedded advertising.

All these activities are aiming to create a brand image which will sell to the target group. We will now look at some more of the ways in which organisations create and develop an audience. This will give you an introduction to some of the marketing strategies they use.

Target groups

These are the particular audience chosen for the product or service. They are defined in terms of the work they do, their gender, their earning/spending power, their age, and their socio-economic grouping. The marketing team builds a profile of the group it is aiming the products at and then tries to target it as an audience. To do this it needs to get precise information about potential customers. One of the ways of obtaining this is through questionnaires.

ACTIVITY

Look at Figure 4.7 on page 82. How do you think the answers to these questions would help the marketing campaign for this games manufacturer?

The information can sometimes be much more personal. Look at Figure 4.8 on pages 83–4, a reader questionnaire for a magazine which is concerned, amongst other things, with computer games. What do the questions tell you about the expected readership of the magazine? Could you build a profile of a typical reader?

This kind of market research suggests that the consumers of media products influence the way they are packaged for them. It raises questions about who is manipulating whom. Does the consumer create the demand which the producer meets? Or does the producer create a need which is met by the product?

Name _____ Age _____
Address _____

_____ Postcode _____

Which consoles or computers do you currently own or have access to?

Do you intend to purchase any of the following in the next 12 months?

Sony PlayStation ☐	CD-ROM equipped PC ☐	Power PC ☐
Sega Saturn ☐	Super Nintendo ☐	Atari Jaguar ☐
Nintendo Ultra 64 ☐	Sega Mega Drive ☐	Jaguar CD-ROM ☐
PC ☐	Game Boy ☐	Amiga ☐
Neo Geo CD ☐	Apple Macintosh ☐	Other (Please state)

Which factor(s) most influence your decision to purchase a game?

Reviews ☐	Promotional Offer ☐	
Advertising ☐	Gift ☐	
Recommendation ☐	In-store Display ☐	
Packaging ☐	Other ☐	

Where do you normally purchase games?

Specialist Chain (i.e. Game, Future Zone etc.)	☐
Non-Specialist Chain (i.e. WH Smiths, Dixons, PC World, HMV etc.)	☐
Specialist Independent	☐
Other	

What is your favourite genre of game?

Beat-em-up ☐	Flight Sim ☐	First Person Perspectives ☐
Arcade ☐	Space Sim ☐	Puzzle ☐
RPG ☐	God Games ☐	Platform ☐
Strategy/War Games☐	Driving Sims ☐	Sports ☐

Thank you for taking the time in completing this postcard.

FIG 4.7 *This games software firm encouraged people to fill in its questionnaire by making it part of a competition*

ACTIVITY

MAKING A GAME
Look at Figure 4.9 on pages 85–9, which shows the front cover and sample pages from the *Ba Boom* comic.

- Design a questionnaire to go out with this first edition which will help to identify the target group and make sure that the approach is appropriate.
- Design a storyboard for a new computer game based on the characters.
- Make suggestions for some marketing events to promote the new game.

What you have learnt

❶ How to use a focus group to carry out research into the uses and pleasures of a media product.

❷ The techniques involved in the marketing of a media product to a specified audience.

❸ That the question of effects is a complicated one and is concerned with the relationship between the media organisation and the audience.

❹ That audiences may actively share ideas about what makes games good and make suggestions to improve the games. They are not simply passive consumers.

Reader Questionnaire

First, some questions about this issue of SFX.

1. How often do you intend to read SFX?

☐ I'm going to subscribe
☐ Every issue
☐ Almost always (at least 3 in every 4 issues)
☐ Regularly (between 1 and 3 in every 4 issues)
☐ Occasionally (less than 1 in every 4 issues)

2. How interesting did you find the following sections of SFX, from 5 (very interesting) to 0 (not at all interesting)?

☐ Strange Tales
☐ Tank Girl
☐ Doctor Who
☐ Iain M Banks
☐ Creature Workshop
☐ Couch Potato
☐ Yesterday's Heroes
☐ Film reviews
☐ TV reviews
☐ Video reviews
☐ Book reviews
☐ Comic reviews
☐ New Media reviews
☐ Toy & Model reviews

3. Mark this issue's cover out of 10.

____ /10

4. Roughly how much of this issue of SFX did you read or look at?

☐ Cover to cover
☐ More than three quarters
☐ About half to three quarters
☐ About a quarter to a half
☐ Less than a quarter

5. How long did you spend reading this issue of SFX?

☐ Three hours or more
☐ Two to three hours
☐ One to two hours
☐ Less than one hour

6. How many people, including yourself, are likely to read this copy of SFX?

☐ 9 or more
☐ 6-8
☐ 4-5
☐ 2-3
☐ 1

7. What will you do with this copy of SFX when you've read it?

☐ Keep it for reference
☐ Pass it on to someone else
☐ Throw it away

8. Which other magazines do you read?

☐ Empire
☐ Premiere (UK)
☐ Premiere (US)
☐ Q
☐ Select
☐ GQ
☐ Arena
☐ Esquire
☐ Edge
☐ .net
☐ Wired
☐ Starburst
☐ Dreamwatch
☐ TV Zone
☐ Starlog
☐ Doctor Who Monthly
☐ Other (please specify below)

_____

9. How interested are you in these different areas that SFX covers? Mark from 5 (very interested) to 0 (not at all interested).

☐ Space adventure movies (e.g. Star Wars)
☐ Sci-fi/horror movies (e.g. Alien)
☐ "Serious" SF movies (e.g. 2001)
☐ Fantasy movies (e.g. Last Action Hero)
☐ Current SF & fantasy TV (e.g. The X-Files)
☐ Cult & classic SF/fantasy TV (e.g. The Prisoner)
☐ Hard SF novels (e.g. Neuromancer)
☐ Soft SF novels (e.g. Any film or TV related novel)
☐ Fantasy novels (e.g. Thomas Covenant novels)
☐ SF/horror novels (e.g. Clive Barker)
☐ SF/fantasy humour novels (e.g. Terry Pratchett)
☐ Superhero comics (e.g. X-Men)
☐ "Mature readers" comics (e.g. Sandman)
☐ Computer and video games
☐ SF toys and models
☐ Special effects/behind-the-scenes stuff
☐ Star interviews

10. Which of these statements do you most agree with?

☐ 1. I'm a science fiction fan! I go and see nearly all the new SF/fantasy films, read a lot of SF books, buy/rent lots of science fiction videos, and attend conventions.

☐ 2. I'm quite into science fiction. I go and see the big films, read a number of books and magazines about it, but I'm not really into the fan scene, and rarely (if ever) attend conventions.

☐ 3. I'm a casual fan. I'm interested in science fiction among a number of other things. I also read other sorts of books, and am interested in other types of films and TV shows.

FIG 4.8

Reader Questionnaire

☐ 4. I'm not really a fan at all, but I do quite like The X-Files.

11. What were your favourite three SF/fantasy films of the last 12 months?

1. _____
2. _____
3. _____

12. What were your three favourite SF/fantasy TV shows of the last 12 months?

1. _____
2. _____
3. _____

13. What were your three favourite SF/fantasy books of the last 12 months?

1 _____
2 _____
3 _____

14. For what reasons do you buy SF books, or choose to go and see SF movies? (Please tick whichever ones are relevant.)

☐ Magazine review
☐ TV programme
☐ Newspaper article
☐ Word of mouth
☐ Friend's recommendation
☐ Advertising
☐ Fan of author/director/etc.
☐ Other (please state)

_____
_____

15. How did you hear of SFX?

☐ Advert in computer magazine
☐ Advert in other type of magazine
☐ News story in magazine
☐ Newspaper
☐ On radio/TV

☐ Word of mouth
☐ Other (please state)

_____
_____

16. What subjects would you like to see more of in future issues of SFX?

_____
_____
_____
_____
_____
_____

17. Was this issue of SFX:
☐ Much better than you expected?
☐ Better than you expected?
☐ About the same as you expected?
☐ Not quite as good as you expected?
☐ A lot worse than you expected?

18 What one thing could we do to improve SFX?

_____
_____
_____
_____
_____
_____
_____
_____

The following questions are about your lifestyle. The answers are strictly confidential, and simple help us a build up a profile of our readership.

19. Do you have a bank and/or building society current account?

☐ Yes ☐ No

20. When did you open your latest current account?

☐ In the last six months
☐ In the last 12 months

☐ 1-2 years ago
☐ More than 2 years ago

21. Which of the following credit/charge cards do you have?

☐ Access/Mastercard
☐ Visa
☐ American Express
☐ Diner's Club
☐ Others (please state)

_____
_____

22. Roughly how many of the following music "stuff" have you bought in the last year?

	Albums	Singles
More than 7	☐	☐
Between 4 and 6	☐	☐
Between 1 and 3	☐	☐
None	☐	☐

23. What types of music do you prefer?

☐ Dance
☐ Rap/hip-hop
☐ Heavy metal
☐ Rave/jungle
☐ House/techno
☐ Reggae/ragga
☐ Indie
☐ Rock
☐ Jazz
☐ Soul
☐ Pop/chart
☐ Classical
☐ Other (please state)

24. What was your favourite band/performer last year?

_____
_____
_____

25. How often do you visit the cinema?

FIG 4.8 *continued*

FIG 4.9

Privacy

- Do you keep a diary?
- Do you keep copies of letters that friends send to you?
- If you tell a friend about something that is worrying you, would you feel let down if you suddenly heard that everyone in school was talking about you?

If your answer to the above questions is yes, you may understand why some famous people dislike the media so much. Things which people think of as private, such as love affairs, parties and relationships, often end up in newspaper columns. Such private matters become news if a person is famous, so that elite status makes a story newsworthy and gives it a news value.

Some people would argue that such interest in private lives is just an excuse for us to be nosey, whilst the press would argue that we have a right to know about politicians who depend on our votes for power, stars who need our loyalty to sustain careers, and sportspeople who should set a good example to young people. What is your attitude?

In the past the press have not always published everything they knew about a person. For example, in the 1930s the then Prince of Wales was developing a friendship with a divorced American woman, Mrs Simpson, but the press did not report as much as they could have about that relationship. Contrast this with the coverage of the Prince and Princess of Wales in modern times. We have been given many more details of the life of royalty and have seen their frailties under a microscope far more than in any other era. It is as well to remember that the media would not pursue these stories so relentlessly if they were not read so avidly by their readership. *The Sun* is a newspaper which is well known for pursuing the details of private lives and it remains Britain's best-selling newspaper.

ACTIVITY

In pairs, look at the following scenarios and decide whether you think the stories should be followed up and published. Make sure you jot down reasons for your choices. When you have decided which stories you think are important for the public to know about, put them in order of priority. Be prepared to defend your choices.

1. A well-known British actor has been arrested for having sex in his car with a prostitute. The actor's star image is based on characteristics of innocence and timidity.

2. A minister in the government is found to be having an affair with his secretary who is now pregnant. He has in the past spoken out against single mothers, accusing them of being a drain on society.

3. A famous television comedian has been seen frequenting gay pubs. A tip-off has told you he may have gay tendencies himself.

4. The Princess of Wales is going on a skiing holiday with her sons, but has asked not to be disturbed by the press.

5. Looking through old police records, it is found that an MP as a student in the 1970s was convicted on a drugs charge of possessing cannabis.

6. An athlete in the British Olympic team has been seen with a well-known drug dealer for sportspeople.

7. An old flame of the Prime Minister has some love letters to tell of their relationship.

8. A private note from a judge to a friend describes the Home Secretary as an idiot.

9. The lover of a convicted murderer has stories to tell about the man's early life.

10. A well-known soap star is expecting a baby, but has refused to name the father as it is a private matter for her.

Compare your lists and nominate a spokesperson out of each pair to present your choices.

News gathering

It is not only the nature of stories which has come under scrutiny in recent years, but also methods of news gathering. Most respectable journalists would not subscribe to some methods which are most criticised.

ACTIVITY

Consider as a class the following methods:
❶ use of camera lenses which enable the photographer to be a long way away from the subject so that the subject does not know he or she is being photographed
❷ use of timing devices on cameras so that the photographer need not be even there as long as he or she knows that the subject will appear at a certain time
❸ use of computer graphics so as to change photographs, insert other people, or bring people closer together.
What curbs would you introduce?

It is often said that the camera cannot lie but, as you know from your work on cropping and montage, the truth can be manipulated in photographs. It is now much easier to do with modern computer techniques.

ACTIVITY

Look through a newspaper(s) in small groups and decide whether the photographs you have in front of you:
- are from archive material, i.e. not taken for the particular story
- have been taken on the spot for this purpose
- have been cropped, in your opinion
- are open to interpretation if the caption is changed
- are juxtaposed with other photographs so that the real meaning comes from the juxtaposition rather than the single image.

FIG 4.10 *How has the photographer created the meaning of this image?*

Constraints

The media do not have as much power as people think. What they report is in fact controlled by the law itself. Remember this is just as true for you when you produce media texts as it is for the media.

ACTIVITY

In pairs, read through the following scenarios. In your opinion would they be allowed to be published? If not, why not?
❶ A British spy wants to sell his memoirs to a Sunday newspaper giving details of British intelligence strategies.
❷ A newspaper describes the suspect in a murder case as the murderer whilst the court case is going on.

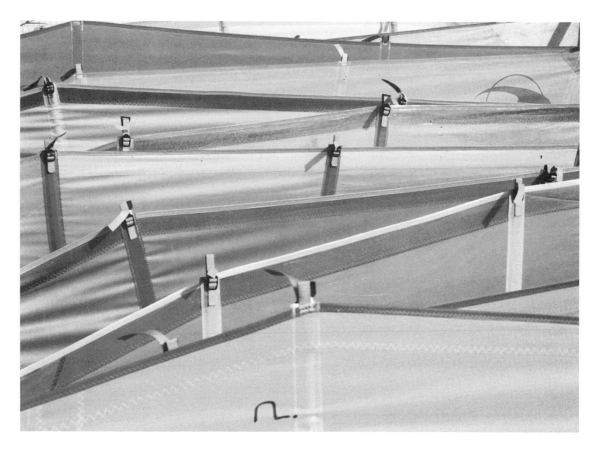

FIG 4.11 *What is this?*

3 A famous politician is said to be gay by another party.
4 A journalist interviews a terrorist who is wanted throughout the world.
5 A famous photographer is to be prosecuted by the police for taking obscene photographs. The photographs have been offered to the newspaper by an anonymous source.

In fact all these stories are highly suspect as they could all be accused of breaking British laws. Here are the laws which govern the publication of printed material. Look again at the suggested stories and say why an editor would be foolish to print them.

Laws which govern the news

The Official Secrets Act, 1911 and 1920 Those who work in the Civil Service are not supposed to reveal any information which is bound up with their jobs. The government decides what is secret and for how long the secret should be kept.

Contempt of Court British courts work on the principle that everyone is innocent until proven guilty, so nothing should appear in the paper which could prejudice justice.

Libel It is illegal to print material which suggests a person is not fit to be trusted or encourages people to hate or make fun of an individual. Obviously it is not right to print things which are not true or based only on hearsay.

Obscene Publications Act This prevents the publication of obscene material and anything which can corrupt, harm or offend.

The Race Relations Act Statements which are threatening, abusive or insulting and which are likely to cause hatred against a racial group are covered by this act.

D notices The government has the power to put these on programmes or newspaper articles. They are requests to the editor not to publish certain stories. The editor has to decide whether it is worth offending the government or whether to go along with the request and keep a good relationship.

The British media, then, cannot broadcast or publish anything they want to. There has to be a balance between:

- the rights of individuals
- a sense of right and wrong
- national security.

The voluntary code

In recent years a whole series of controversies about reporting have emerged because in Great Britain we do not have a privacy law. Many people feel that there should be more controls. In 1992 the Calcutt Report suggested more controls and the setting up of a tribunal to judge whether papers had broken the rules. In response to this newspapers came up with their own voluntary code of behaviour:

- the right to privacy can be broken only if there is a legitimate public interest
- public interest is different to the interest shown by the public
- technological eavesdropping can only be justified by public interest
- news gathering should be sensitive to personal circumstances.

ACTIVITY

MAKING THE RULES

❶ Make a report on the power of the press, giving a clear set of recommendations on how you think newspapers can improve the way they report private matters, or defending the way they behave now.

❷ Construct a letter or a short radio item giving your views on the way the press invade the privacy of particular individuals.

❸ Do some vox pop interviews which explore responses to a set of questions about the freedom of the press. Edit these into a short radio item.

What you have learnt

❶ *There are events which cannot be reported by the media.*

❷ *There are events which are reported by the media which cause great controversy.*

❸ *Privacy is an issue which is largely left to the media to make their minds up about.*

❹ *There is controversy about stories which are published in the public interest.*

Further thoughts

This chapter has used another three case studies to open out further aspects of the relationships between audiences and organisations. In the first unit the emphasis is on an approach through a well-known media character, Batman, who has attracted fans ever since his first appearance in a comic. It also introduces you to another concept which is important for the media student: **intertextuality**. In simple terms, this means that no text can be read without reference to other texts. The original Batman draws on the conventions of the super-hero Superman, and even he draws on other stories of people who have a double life and stories of human beings with supernatural powers. You can also connect a character like Batman to other media productions: the most obvious one is the vigilante detective. Your work on television crime dramas may help you develop ideas like these, or indeed your work on a favourite star, like Clint Eastwood.

Fans make a point of finding out everything they can about their chosen media product and are very powerful in keeping a character such as Batman alive. However, fans by themselves are not enough. The products still have to attract mass audiences and so have to change and develop. Different producers have made Batman relevant to the concerns of their own age in their attempt to attract an audience: the character can represent different social concerns and be targeted at different kinds of audiences.

The second unit explores the idea further that certain groups are targeted by the media. It is a very common notion that young children are influenced by the media. In a way this view suggests that they are being subjected to some extremely dangerous and unpleasant material over which they have no control. In contrast to this there is the media theory of uses and gratifications, which suggests that audiences make use of media productions to gratify the need for information, for a sense of identity, for social interaction, and for entertainment and diversion. In such a view of the audience, the consumer takes a much more active role. You will find more on this theory in Part 2 of the book. Your research may also have given you some insight into the idea that the consumer is by no means as uncritical as is often supposed. Finally, some questions may have been raised in your mind about whether, in fact, young children are the target audience as is commonly supposed.

The media issue which is the basis of the third unit begins to open up the question of who controls the media and how these controls opera te. It raises questions about key issues in our society – about rights and responsibilities. In contrast to the previous two units it is based on factual material. In this kind of work you can learn to argue for your viewpoint which is also an important media skill; we all have opinions but media students have the examples, evidence and knowledge to back them up.

5

Access to the media

Entertaining yourself: you and your video

The biggest selling item of electrical hardware for the home in the 1980s was a video player. Nearly everyone living in a city, town or village now has some access to video rental or shops which sell videos. Most places have a specialist video shop for purchase or rental. Some remote places still have mobile vans, though these have tended to be replaced by garages, off-licences and grocery shops. The change has been quite recent: in the 1970s videos were far less common. Some people are suggesting that the day of the video will be over by the end of the millennium in 2000 AD, although you will remember that people said radio was dead when television started.

So the home video market is a good place to investigate further the uses of technology in our everyday lives and to explore the claims that new technologies increase our choices and give us more control over the way we entertain ourselves. We are in the middle of an entertainment revolution which will evolve in new ways, especially through the use of digital technology. However, the issues raised by the new technologies can be explored through a case study of what is now an everyday part of our experience of the media: the home video.

Discuss the following statements. Do you agree with them?

1 Video recorders give you more control over what and when you decide to view because you don't have to wait around all evening for your favourite programme.
2 You have much more choice about the films you can watch and when and where you watch them.
3 You can produce your own video programmes by using a video camera and so make your own entertainment in the home.

Your discussion of statement 1 will have involved you in a discussion about **time shifting**. Your work on statement 2 will mean you have been thinking about **playback practices**. Your discussion of statement 3 will mean you have been thinking about **production practices**. Each of these is interesting to explore further. You can start by investigating your group's use and experience of home video.

Time shifting

Here are a few questions to start you off. Some of these are quantitative questions so that you can present your information in graphical and/or statistical form. Others are qualitative, seeking opinions which you may want to present in other visual forms like a poster or leaflet.

You may want to ask other kinds of questions as well, so think about what you are trying to find out and organise your research. You always need to think about the people who are going to look at your research.

1 How many video machines are there in your home?
   (a) 0 **(b)** 1 **(c)** more

2 How many video cassettes do you have for recording purposes?
   (a) 0 **(b)** 5 **(c)** more

These questions are useful in identifying people who you might want to talk to in more detail.

3 Where is the video machine in your home?
   (a) main room **(b)** bedroom
   (c) other (specify)

4 Where are the video cassettes stored?
   (a) by the machine **(b)** in a bedroom
   (c) in a special unit **(d)** other

These two questions might be useful for exploring how people actually use their videos.

5 Who has access to the video cassettes?
   (a) adults only **(b)** teenagers
   (c) young children

This might help with investigations into how parents/teenagers feel about the effects of videos.

6 When do people watch programmes recorded off-air?
   Adults **(a)** during the day **(b)** early evening **(c)** late at night
   Teenagers **(a)** during the day **(b)** early evening **(c)** late at night
   Children **(a)** during the day **(b)** early evening **(c)** late at night

This question is useful for identifying different patterns of use.

7 What kind of programmes do you record?
   (a) drama **(b)** sport **(c)** documentary
   (d) news **(e)** music **(f)** game shows
   (g) films

This question may be helpful in exploring gender/genre issues.

8 Who of your closest relations knows how to programme the video to record off-air?
   (a) father **(b)** mother **(c)** guardian
   (d) sister **(e)** brother **(f)** best friend

You will find this question helpful in exploring gender/age/technology issues.

Some issues to do with time shifting

In 1976 a lawyer for the Walt Disney Corporation said 'the videotape machine would be used to steal our property'.

- Do you agree that when you record off-air you are stealing someone else's property?
- Which law protects the producer of a media text from unlawful copying?
- Why would the makers of programmes and films argue that their rights should be protected and they should be paid a fee for making the programme available for recording?
- Why would makers of video machines argue the opposite?
- How could you stop people from recording programmes they wanted to see?
- What kind of a society would it be if we could be prevented from recording off-air?

Most research shows that by the mid-80s the average VCR owner spent about two and a half hours recording. However, they spent four hours playing tapes. What would be the reason for this? Is it like you?

Playback practices

Your research has probably shown you what you already knew: namely, that most people now use pre-recorded material which they rent or buy more than they record material themselves.

However, the growth in availability of pre-recorded material was much slower than the growth in the ownership of the VCR and it is only now, perhaps, that we are aware of the video rental and purchase market. One reason for this was that the producers of films were anxious to keep control of their property and resisted attempts to give more access to their products. Here are some of the things they tried to do:

- **Prohibit rentals of films which companies had purchased and promote the sales of videodiscs which could not be copied.** Could the new owner of the film rent copies of what was now personal property?
- **Sell more of their films but get a bigger share of the cost of the rental.** Video dealers resisted this and won. How could the distributor keep track of the number of times a film was rented without the co-operation of the dealers?
- **Fit all VCRs with an anti-copying device.** How expensive would the video recorders be?
- **Produce video cassettes that destroyed themselves after a specific number of plays.** Would this prevent pirate copying?

Copying of blockbuster films in Far Eastern countries has become very big business and the USA has threatened trade sanctions against governments who do not try to control pirate copying.

Video rental outlets

Perhaps the best way to stop pirate copying is to control the distribution network. If you control the places where your products are sold or rented you control the profits to be made.

Who owns the video rental outlet: a private person who gets video films from a lot of different sources or a manager who runs the shop for a large chain? In the early days it would have been a private individual, but now it is more likely to be a manager employed by or franchised to a chain.

Who owns the chain? The owners are usually also the people who distribute the films. What happened in the 1980s was that the major Hollywood film producers moved into the video rental business, opening new chains of outlets for their products and squeezing out the independent owners.

Most towns now have at least one Blockbuster video chain store. Does yours? If not, what does it have? Can you explain why?

ACTIVITY

Investigate your group's use of video rental outlets.
❶ Survey the videos of feature films that your group rents in a specified time period (the bigger the group, the less time you will need for a decent sample) by noting the titles and the supplier.
❷ Categorise the titles using this list of suppliers: Paramount, Disney, Warner, MCA, Columbia, MGM, Twentieth Century Fox.
❸ What evidence would you have for saying that local video rentals are dominated by these major producers?

Marketing strategies

ACTIVITY

Look at Figure 5.1 on page 98, a promotion page featured in the *Observer* at the end of 1995.
❶ Who is paying for the promotion? Why?
❷ The *Observer* newspaper is targeted at particular social groups. Thinking about this, discuss the use of:
   (a) downmarket alternative (paragraph 1)
   (b) a top leisure pursuit (paragraph 1)
   (c) users wanting the same control over films that CDs provide for music (paragraph 2).
❸ What are:
   (a) surround sound
   (b) high-definition wide screen TV
   (c) digital technology

Video Daze

Here is the first of our comprehensive four-week guide to the exciting world of home entertainment

Where once video was seen as a downmarket alternative to the cinema, it's now central to film culture. More than 600 million video recorders have been manufactured throughout the world and it's become an integral part of Home Entertainment. Blockbuster Video, the largest rental chain in the UK, has grown rapidly in recent years. According to its European Vice President Nigel Travis, 'we have 4 million members and aim to reach 85 per cent of the population. We have worked to make video a top leisure pursuit, rather than one of last resort.'

Films account for 95 per cent of video rentals and more than a third of video purchases. 'Home Cinema is the fastest growing area of the home entertainment revolution,' argues Sony UK. Surround sound brings the cinematic effects in films such as *Batman Forever* straight into the living room, while high-definition widescreen TV show-

cases the growing number of special directors' cuts. And with users wanting the same control over films that CDs provide for music, the industry is looking forward to the development of digital technology. In future sections we'll be looking at The New Viewer, Interactive Games, and The New Cinema.

But here are the basics:

BROADEN YOUR OUTLOOK:
Available for the last three years, widescreen TV works brilliantly with the likes of *Apocalypse Now* and *Bladerunner*. The promoters claim that its letterbox appearance reflects 'our natural field of vision'. But on normal programmes, the zoom function on some models can have a terrifying squash-and-stretch effect.

THE SOUNDS OF TODAY:
The key new technology is called Dolby Pro-Logic. In addition to the left and right channels common to standard stereo, the system

provides complete surround sound. To achieve this you need to position additional speakers throughout the room, though JVC has developed a new 3D-Phonic system which attempts to create the effect of surround sound with in-built speakers. Television programmes such as *Cracker* are now being broadcast in stereo, but for full use you need a Nicam stereo video to get access to a range of stereo movies.

THE FUTURE IS DIGITAL:
The video industry is attempting to apply CD technology to film products. Laser discs were launched in the early Eighties, providing exceptional picture quality and superb extra features. More recently, Philips have launched CDi, which enables music, games and video CDs to be played from one unit (see the compact version above).

The problem with both formats is that feature films cannot be fitted onto one disc. The great advantage of Digital Video Disc (DVD), now being developed jointly by the main video manufacturers (after a recent industry agreement designed to avoid the disastrous battle between VHS and Beta), is that one disc can store an entire movie.

The format provides far more versatility than VHS, though the first models will not be available in the UK until at least 1997.

Double Feature

You can choose any two films from the Blockbuster Video Movie Collection. Below, Philip French suggests two alternative pairs

The African Queen (1951) and The Piano (1993)
In these two poised, psychological adventure stories, American actresses (Katharine Hepburn and Holly Hunter) impersonate genteel British women in remote corners of the Empire on the brink of war. Both take up with, and are liberated by boozy tough guys who've gone native (Humphrey Bogart and Harvey Keitel).

The Last Of The Mohicans and Unforgiven (both 1992)
A fine pre-Western and a great Western offering different views of the frontier experience. In *Last Of The Mohicans*, Daniel Day-Lewis runs gracefully through the forests of 18th-century New England as Hawkeye, the idealistic scout serving the British. In *Unforgiven*, Clint Eastwood as an ageing ex-gunfighter rides none too surely across the bleak plains of the late 19th-century West to kill for money.

2 for 1 offer

The Observer has joined forces with Blockbuster Video to offer you the chance to make your next video rental a double feature. Rent any movie from the Blockbuster Video Movie Collection and you can borrow another one for no extra cost.

Here is how to take part:
Cut out the coupon below.
Take it to any Blockbuster Video store any day next week.
Select a video from the Blockbuster Video Movie Collection.
Choose another video from the Movie Collection to borrow free.
Present your coupon at the cash desk with both your videos.
If you are not already a Blockbuster Video member you will need to join free of charge by showing two forms of ID (eg drivers license, bank statements).
You can keep your videos out for up to two nights.
There will be a coupon in the Observer each week for the next three weeks, so you can enjoy four free videos all together.
Each coupon remains valid for one week only.

Terms and Conditions 1. Instructions above form part of the terms and conditions 2. Only one rental per membership per week from the Movie Collection 3. Videos borrowed under this offer must be returned within the normal rental period 4. Not to be used with any other offer 5. Offer not available in Ireland 6. No cash alternative.

- -

Double Feature: Rent one get one free

56000300004

the Observer

Valid until 18.11

FIG 5.1

(d) Dolby Pro-Logic

(e) Nicam stereo video?

You will be able to find information in any of the major retailers like Curries, Dixons and Comet or in advertising material.

❹ What was the battle between VHS and Beta? Who won?

❺ Use your own video store to find out which of the production companies owns the rights to the films mentioned in the promotion:

(a) *Batman Forever*

(b) *Apocalypse Now*

(c) *Unforgiven*

(d) *Bladerunner*

(e) *The African Queen*

(f) *The Piano*

(g) *The Last of the Mohicans*

What are your conclusions?

❻ Why would the growing number of special directors' cuts be important to both the audience for this promotion and the producers of the films concerned?

❼ Explain why there is a bar code on the cut-out section in the bottom right-hand corner of the page?

Production practices

Camcorders and other video systems have been used mostly to document family activities. One view is that camcorders are replacing the camera as the main way of recording major family

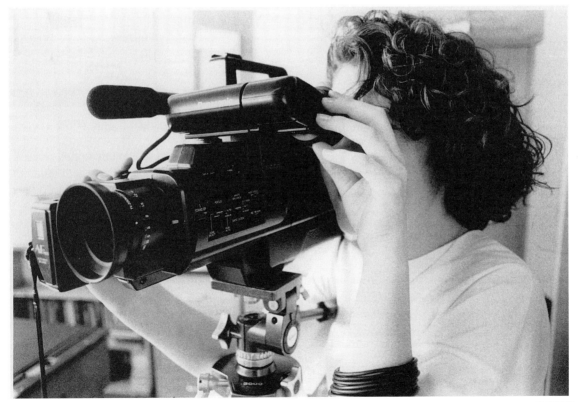

© *MEW*

FIG 5.2 *Production practices*

occasions such as births, marriages and holidays. If true, you are probably in a very pivotal position in this process. It is likely that you have records of yourself in both photograph and film form; this would be more unusual for your parents.

ACTIVITY

RESEARCHING MEDIA HISTORY

Find out, using a survey technique, how an older generation (parents or grandparents or similarly aged adults) and a group of people your own age know how they looked when they were children. Present your findings in an interesting way to an adult audience and/or a teenage audience.

MEDIA FUTURES

How will you document the most important parts of your life in the future? What are the advantages/disadvantages of photographs and videos for documenting your family life?

MEDIA NOW

As a group, discuss the following questions:
- Who 'owns' the camera/camcorder?
- Where are the images stored? Do you need permission to use them?
- When are the images used? Would these change according to where you were?
- What happens to the images when the person(s) who owns them die?

Recording real life

Family video recordings of real life events can make popular viewing material. For example, the television programme *You've Been Framed* is based on funny videos of domestic mishaps sent in by the audience.

ACTIVITY

❶ What is your favourite video clip from the programme? Try to describe it to someone who has not seen it.

❷ Record the programme (or one like it). Try to work out:

    (a) who sent in the video clip, where they lived, and why they might have sent it

    (b) what this tells you about where the programme makers want to sell their programme

    (c) the different categories of the clips, e.g. animal, children, etc.

❸ What kind of clips will *not* be used in the programme, do you think? Suggest good and bad ideas which could be considered for the programme.

There is also an increasing use of video recordings on television from people who witness crimes or unlawful activities. These people are sometimes called 'video vigilantes'. What do you think this term means?

ACTIVITY

In pairs, discuss the following uses of the camcorder:

❶ In the Rodney King trial in Los Angeles much of the controversy concerned the use of amateur video shot at the scene of the beating of Rodney King, a black man, at the hands of the police.

❷ Some people try to sell footage of crimes they have videoed to the authorities.

❸ Some local authorities, police authorities and businesses sell footage taken by their video surveillance units to media organisations for use in documentary programmes.

❹ It is possible to put video footage that we take onto the Worldwide Web.

What you have learnt

❶ *All new media technologies make promises that they will give more freedom of choice and greater access to the consumer.*

❷ *All media organisations seek to control the use of their products by law if they can, or if not by other means.*

❸ *New technologies raise as many new issues for the consumer as they bring benefits.*

❹ *The new technologies affect the ways in which we record ourselves and our histories.*

Walt Disney: not a Mickey Mouse affair

Almost every person in the British Isles has some knowledge of the film work of Walt Disney, but did you know that the Disney Corporation sees the 1990s as 'The Disney Decade'? This unit explores how you and everyone else you know is involved in 'the magical world of Disney' and how you are part of a worldwide organisation devoted to making money for its shareholders, now and in the future.

How far has the Disney culture penetrated your life?

ACTIVITY

PERSONAL QUIZ

❶ How many characters from Disney films can you name?

❷ Who is your favourite Disney character? What features of the character make it instantly recognisable?

❸ Do you own any of the films as videos? Do you watch them any more?

❹ Have you seen the latest Disney film? Where or in what circumstances did you see it? Was it on video or at the cinema?

❺ How old were you when you saw (if you have) *Aladdin, The Lion King, Snow White, Bambi, A Hundred and One Dalmations, Cinderella, Beauty and the Beast*?

❻ Have you ever had any Disney merchandising?

❼ How many Disney merchandising items can you name?

❽ Have you ever been involved in a Disney promotion, at MacDonalds for instance?

❾ Have you ever been to Disneyland Paris or to Disneyland or Disneyworld?

❿ Have you ever bought anything from a Disney shop?

Compare the results with the rest of the class.

Walt Disney's cartoons are amongst the most popular films ever made. Mickey Mouse is the most famous cartoon character of all time. Can you draw Mickey or Donald Duck, or both?

ACTIVITY

In small groups, discuss the following questions:
1. Do you think you ever grow out of Disney?
2. Why do you think Disney films are so memorable and popular?
3. Disney films are sometimes criticised. Do you agree or disagree with the following statements?
   - The heroines are stereotypes of conventional 'pretty' girls and are a bit 'wet'.
   - Although the animation is brilliant, the stories themselves are sentimental and escapist.

Team Disney

Most of your opinions will be based on your experiences of the animated films. Certainly our approach has focused on these. However, the Disney empire, as you probably already realise, is much bigger than these films. Team Disney is the name of the management team who seek to use the Disney name worldwide for maximum profits. They want you to spend your money on their products and services.

We have broken up the business organisation of Team Disney so that you can investigate where you fit into the Disney business plan.

Film and television

The film library. Lots of Disney films have been made since the 1930s, and in the 1980s and 1990s many have been re-released in video format. There are nearly 200 feature films, about 30 full-length animations and over 500 cartoon shorts.

ACTIVITY

Check out your local supermarket, Woolworths or Blockbuster.
- How many re-releases can you find?
- What classifications do the films have?
- Who are the displays targeted at?
- How (and when) are Disney films advertised on television?

New films. Many new films are made under the Disney label. However, many have appeared under new labels. Buena Vista Home Video, Touchstone and Hollywood Pictures are all Disney labels.

ACTIVITY

What kinds of films can you find in your local video outlet which have any of these labels? Are the film classifications different to those with Disney labels?

Prime-time television. The Disney group make television programmes as well. Programmes which attract the largest audiences and therefore the largest advertising revenue are game shows, cartoons and situation comedies. The American shows are often **syndicated** to Great Britain which means that, to create attractive schedules, British television groups buy programmes or programme concepts. *Home Improvements* is a Disney programme; *Gladiators* is a programme concept (in America it is called *The Challengers*); *The Golden Girls*, an American situation comedy, had a British spinoff called *The Brighton Belles*. Disney also syndicates cartoons in special packages like *Disney Time*.

Can you find examples of other syndicated programmes or programme concepts adapted for British television? Cartoons, game shows and situation comedies are good genres to study. Channel 4 and the Saturday morning schedules of ITV and the BBC are a good place to start. Satellite channels will have lots of examples, although you will need a satellite listings magazine to help you. Do not worry if they are not Disney products.

Theme parks and resorts

Some of you will have been to these and may have photographs, videos and souvenirs.

Disneyworld, Orlando, Florida, USA. This is a huge complex which needs more than one holiday to visit (according to *The Holiday Programme*). It has the magic kingdom, the Epcot centre, the Disney/MGM studios theme park, a night-time entertainment centre, a shopping village, a conference centre, a campground, golf courses and water parks. It is developing new facilities all the time and the designers are constantly looking at new ways to entertain you. They have invented a new science called imagineering. What do you think this is?

Disneyland, Tokyo, Japan. Disneyland was opened in 1983 as a franchise and has been a huge success in Japan.

Disneyland, Paris, France. This opened in 1992 and by 1994 it was the biggest paid tourist attraction in Europe.

Explore how the Disney Corporation seek to attract you by researching the travel brochures that they produce for their theme parks and resorts.
- What kinds of images do they use?
- How are the facilities described?

- What can you learn of the target groups that they seek to attract?

Travel programmes on television will also be a good source of material to analyse.

Consumer products

Every Disney character, film, song and piece of music is licensed. This means that you cannot use it for any commercial purpose without the permission of the Disney Corporation. Disney will only license (i.e. let other people make products using Disney material or images) those who pay to do so. Disney is one of the toughest companies in terms of enforcing its copyright. It is also the most successful merchandising company in the world. Often the merchandising can make more money than the film.

Some key areas for mini investigations are given below.

Comic books, children's books and other printed material
- How much does your group have?
- How many can you find in local libraries, book shops, supermarkets and newsagents?

Audio recordings, records, CDs and musical scores for different instruments
- How many can you find in a local newsagent, record or music shop?

Retail outlets in major cities and mail-order catalogues
- What kinds of merchandising can you find related to either your favourite Disney character or the latest Disney film?

Disney educational productions
- Disney produces films, videos and film strips for schools and libraries. Check what your local library or junior school has.
- It also produces school and playgroup equipment. Does your local playgroup, infant school or crèche have any?

Disney software licensing

- Disney licenses software producers to produce spinoff games. Check what games linked to Disney creations are available in your local games store.

All groups should report back their findings.

Concept drawing

It is very difficult to match the quality of the Disney animations which require a huge investment of expertise, time, resources and technical skills: the production values ensure products of the highest specification. However, anyone can have good ideas and think of ways of communicating those ideas. A good way of understanding the ways in which Disney films are made is to consider the individual tasks which make the films so successful:

- creating concept sketches for a new Disney character
- writing a plot summary or adaptation of an existing fairy story
- writing song lyrics
- scripting the voice-over for a sequence
- planning/designing merchandising ideas.

You can also challenge the typical situations, characters and ways of telling the story so that these can be made more visible. For example, the magazine *Mad* uses **parody** to expose the assumptions and working practices of the media. By using humour it hopes to reveal alternative ways of looking at media products and practices. In a recent example it challenged a Disney production which you may know: *Pocahontas*. It started by renaming the central character Pokeyhontas, suggesting perhaps that there was some hocus pocus about the fact that the central character, who was an Indian princess, became a very American young woman/princess in the film. It also exposed the facts that John Smith, the white man who marries Pocahontas, was much older than he was represented in the film and that in our society Pocahontas would be too young to marry. The Disney version missed this out. So, the story which was presented as a typical love story by Disney was made fun of in a black-and-white comic strip with low production values. It reveals how such popular films could be made very differently and probably more controversially.

ACTIVITY

Choose your favourite Disney character and/or situation and try to use parody to expose the conventions which control the representation.
   Here is an idea if you are stuck:

   Snow White leads the seven dwarfs in a national miners' strike rather than cooking and cleaning the house for them.

You will need to outline the main parts of the story as you did in *Beauty and the Beast* and rearrange them into a new narrative. Decide on:

- which bits can be parodied
- new character profiles for the main characters
- a new form: story, comic strip, radio play.

What you have learnt

1 *A global organisation like Disney expands its commercial activities not only in the USA but also across the whole world.*

2 *Its activities are diverse and can affect whole areas of our lives.*

3 *Marketing Disney products is a huge business.*

4 *Parody can be a good way of undermining the dominant system of representation to see how it has been constructed. The typical points of view which are represented are American.*

Alternative publishing

When we speak of media, we tend to mean the mass media – products which reach large numbers of people and are produced by distribution of labour. The Disney enterprise, for instance, employs huge numbers of people globally in an enormous variety of jobs. Behind the success of the great Disney films are lots of different people with an amazing diversity of skills.

Although magazines are a mass medium, in this category (as in all media products) there is a sub-category of alternative magazines. The term 'alternative' can be used as a description of its means of production and intended audience and/or as a description of its content and messages.

Alternative suggests:

● another choice or option
● a different lifestyle.

Although some people work in alternative media as a means of getting into mainstream publishing, many enjoy the benefits of working on small-scale projects and value the hands-on experience it offers them.

ACTIVITY

In pairs, discuss whether you have come across or been involved with (as either a consumer or producer) the following alternative publications:
  ● a school magazine
  ● a church newsletter
  ● a community paper (e.g. news of your housing estate, neighbourhood watch)
  ● a newsletter or magazine for vegetarians or Friends of the Earth
  ● a fanzine (pop, film, television, sport).
With these examples in mind, try to think of some characteristics that define the alternative press. Here are some examples to help you:
  ● specialist or local interest
  ● small readership compared to mainstream
  ● low budget
  ● co-operative means of production, with no specialisms but everyone contributing.

Connect Press

The best way to understand alternative media is by comparing it with mainstream publishing. Connect Press is an alternative publisher which, during the 1980s, published two magazines of creative writing called *Connections* and *Sinister Women*. In the 1990s, Connect abandoned the magazine format and has instead encouraged writers to publish work by writing on pavements in chalk.

Read the following interview with the editor and jot down what it tells you about the alternative press.

❛ *Interviewer:* How did Connect Press come about?

Editor: I knew lots of people who wrote but who were told by mainstream publishers that their writing did not fit the market and was not commercial enough. I liked what was being written and I thought other people would too.

Interviewer: How did you manage to finance a project like this?

Editor: I started with simple materials and a Gestetner printer which I bought myself, and then I wrote to a range of people asking them to subscribe in advance for three copies. I meant to bring out three copies a year.

Interviewer: How many people were involved?

Editor: About 50. I realised I would need to have a wider distribution than that, so I canvassed book shops in the surrounding area and also health food shops.

Interviewer: That suggests you had an idea of who your audience might be.

Editor: Yes. People who are more interested in content than appearance, ideas rather than how they were presented. I think, looking back, that copies were rather rough and could have been presented in a better way, but at the time I was producing the magazine myself: typing, editing, selecting, printing, distributing.

Interviewer: That must have been exhausting.

Editor: Yes, it was. It was a labour of love.

Interviewer: Does that mean it didn't make any money?

Editor: I don't think alternative magazines do – well it is always a problem. I did break even.

Interviewer: What did you publish?

Editor: First of all I published material of people I knew, but after the magazine appeared in book shops I had a lot of material sent to me. I published if I felt that the work had merit and was dealing with honest emotions.

Interviewer: After four editions you changed to a woman's creative magazine called *Sinister Women*. Why was that?

Editor: There are problems in sustaining magazines when so much work has to be done by so few, in this case one, and there is no financial backing. I asked four women who had contributed to the magazine to form a collective and, since we were all women, we decided to target a female audience. Sinister comes from the Latin word for left, so we were trying to suggest we were alternative in content to other magazines.

Interviewer: How did the collective work?

Editor: We all put the same amount of money into the scheme. We took it in turns to be in charge of an edition; we all contributed to each edition and split the work load. This worked better, but where there is no distribution of labour and people don't know where their own job begins and ends there can be difficulties, squabbles ... I'm sure pop groups and drama groups have similar problems. People disagree ... compromise or don't compromise. It takes a lot of energy and commitment and, in my experience, it can work for a few projects but becomes hard to sustain. We were only producing 100 copies, but that takes a lot of doing when you have no back up and have to do everything from editing to stapling.

Interviewer: You don't publish magazines any more?

Editor: No, but it was enjoyable. I always say that Connect Press is not dead, it only sleeps. The idea of publishing work on the street is a good one. Artists draw, so why not poets and other writers? Audiences enjoy it – they always stop to read it. You have to get written permission from the council, but they usually give it although they define where you can write. **9**

ACTIVITY

EXAMINING TEXTS

1 Use the interview to make a list of the problems associated with working in the alternative press.

2 Examine the covers and contents pages of *Connections* and the student magazine, *Prophecy*, shown in Figure 5.3 on pages 108–9. What can you learn of the magazines?

3 Compare an alternative magazine with a glossy mainstream magazine.

4 Read the excerpts from *Prophecy* shown in Figure 5.4 on pages 110–13. How do they differ from pages in a glossy magazine?

5 Study the reader questionnaire shown in Figure 5.5 on page 114. What in your view is the typical reader profile?

In Great Britain there is a strong tradition of community presses, where publications are designed to give information and/or keep communities together, giving a sense of community service. You may want to become involved with this and help to produce such material.

ACTIVITY

MAKING AN ALTERNATIVE MAGAZINE

1 Choose a minority interest of your own, e.g. vegetarianism, tropical fish, chess, poetry, rock climbing, weight training. Imagine you are going to produce a magazine on this subject. Design the following:

- a cover for your alternative magazine
- a contents page
- an editorial explaining what the magazine is about.

2 Produce something which will be of use for your community or school, such as:

- a calendar using photographs and/or writing of another class to be sold in the community
- a guide to spelling or to option choices which could be distributed at parents' evenings
- a newsletter for your church, chapel or religious group or your youth group.

3 Figure 5.6 shows a picture of a hopeful pop star. What changes would you make to his image? What types of music would you expect him to play? Design a page spread about his likes, dislikes and habits for a teenage alternative magazine.

FIG 5.6

FIG 5.3

Index

FIG 5.4 *Sample pages from* Prophecy *magazine*

CONTENTS.

COVER STORY.

Kevin Edwards reviews the Convention of Merlin, commemorating the 400th anniversary of the master magician himself. Held at Korton Castle in Gloucestershire, it provided a 4 day event set on a stunning scale. It incorporated theatre acts, lectures, and stalls presented with real care and precision. Whether Merlin ever really existed remains a mystery, but the events at Korton Castle prove that real or not he was one of the world's best-known and best loved Wizards. See pages 10+11

3-D Make-It!

Another great idea sent in by a reader. This week we show you how to construct convincing 3-D landscapes which can be used as gaming boards for army miniatures or simply for show. Once again this is a Make-It which does not need specialist materials or specialist skills and can be done by those aged 5-50+. All you do need is a bit of patience and imagination, and the willingness to get up to your armpits in papier mache! If you have a great idea for a Make-It, you can send it to us, with clear, step-by-step instructions to, Make-It, Prophecy, 4-6 Elmslack Road, Carncaster, LA5 LA4. We regret that we are unable to return your suggestions and so it is a good idea to make a photocopy.

A Word from the Editor.

Once again, we have a packed issue for you. Our cover story, the Convention of Merlin, provoked some serious debate amongst the Prophecy team, as various wizard-gurus waved their copies of 'The Once and Future King,' and the 'Encyclopedia of Mythic Fact,' at each other trying to prove whether it was or was not correct to call the convention the four-hundredth anniversary. When we tried to explain to them that they were missing the point, they stomped off to their respective desks still clutching these books and from time to time muttering, 'Yes, but...'

Aside from that, the team have been poring over the new edition of 'Talisman.' In this week's competition we have six games to give away, so try your luck.

Thank you for all the entries to the 'Design the Book-Cover Illustration' competition, from the last issue. We have already had a number of very good entries, but the closing date is not until August the 1st. Remember you don't need to be a brilliant artist to enter - the judges are looking at thoughtful and original design as well as presentation.

Enjoy the issue,

Angela Phillips.

REGULARS

ADDRESS INFORMATION.
If you want to contact us, the Prophecy team, or you want to enter one of the competitions, write to Prophecy, 4-6 Elmslack Road, Carncaster, LANCS LA5 LA4. However if you wish to contact one of the Penfriends, write direct to the address at the base of the letter, not the Prophecy address. If you wish to place a penfriend letter, write to Penfriends, Prophecy, Spindrift House, 25 Westminster Lane, NE5 NE1.

The editor reserves the right to make final decisions on all competition entries. This includes disqualification. For general office enquiries phone 346 2753

GALLERY

This exciting picture has been sent in by one of our younger readers: nine year old Adam White from Hartlepool. The orange ships are called landspeeders, he says, on a ground patrol. Those that are higher above the ground are the upgraded model of the same ship, for better offensive postioning. For sending us such a brilliant picture, Adam will receive a special goody-bag with book and film vouchers, a Prophecy Mug and a mystery prize..... Well done Adam!

DO YOU WANT A PICTURE EXHIBITED ON THE GALLERY PAGE?

You can send us any picture that is related to fantasy or science fiction, in any medium. (If it is 3-Dimensional, please send us a photograph of it.)

Please send pictures which are no larger than A3, preferably A4. We understand that you will often want your work returned, so if you do, please enclose a SAE. Please send us a little bit of information about yourself with your work so we can print something interesting about you too.

DON'T FORGET ....
BOOK-COVER DESIGN COMPETITION.

It is still not too late to enter this great competition. All you have to do is design the cover illustration for Morgan Harvey's novel, "The Singing Stone," which was reviewed last month. However, if you did not get last month's issue of Prophecy, you won't know much about the book and therefore have difficultty designing an appropriate cover. You can write to us for a quick resume, or phone us at the office. This information can be found on the content's page. Entries need to be in by August 1st 1995. First prize is a 100 pound book-voucher and a special hardback edition of Havey's novel with their design. Three runners up will receive a paperback copy of the novel, with their design. Designs should be submitted on A4 paper, front and back cover design on the same page, so you could fold the page in half and have them in the right place.

Sally Ericson of New Framshire Art and Design College sent us this portrait from her project. She is doing a study of faces, expression in context and this is one of the preliminary sketches for a much larger piece. This is not the first time that Sally has had some of her artwork published in Prophecy. If you have issue 7, you will find a picture of Bilbo Baggins that Sally did 3 years ago! Well done, Sally and good luck with the project!

FIG 5.4 *continued*

COMPETITION

TALISMAN - the return!

Everyone has their favourite memory of the wet-weekend-filling wonder-game, which never ceased to amuse your freetime. For some it was the legendary Choose Your Own Adventure Books, that provided endless ours of bending the rules. (don't try and deny you didn't mark the pages in case you made a mistake.)

For others there was Talisman, one of the earliest role-playing fantasy games. More than one generation would have traveled through its perilous land in search of the Crown of Command.

Now, Games Workshop has brought out another edition, with improved characters and involvement. It promises to be an improvement on the previous editions, with further clarifications on the rules.

Games Workshop has also produced a number of extension packs for Talisman which make the original game harder, more exciting and able to take up more table room!

We have six of the new edition Talisman Games to give away. All you have to do is answer the following question:

NAME ANY TWO OF THE FIVE CHARACTERS WITH A NEUTRAL ALIGNMENT.

The first six correct entries pulled out of the hat will recieve the Talisman game. Send your entries to :
Talisman comp, Prophecy, 4-6 Elmslack Road,
Carncaster, LANCS LA5 LA4

The winners of last weeks Eye Of The Beholder competition were:
Anna Humes, Bristol; Colin Mockery, New Jersey, Phillipa Smith, New Quay; Paul Simpson, Stoke, Gillian Austin, Bolton; and Simon Holmes, Cardiff. Well done all of you. Your prizes will be winging their way to you as we speak.

MEDEA

STOCKISTS IN THE UNUSUAL

We now have branches throughout the UK: Manchester, Bolton, Essex, Preston and Kendal. We specialise in crystals, jewellry, sculpture and healing. We also have a wide range of clothes music, posters, books and stationery.

Second-hand original comics can be bought and sold for reasonable prices. We have over 1,500 collector's pieces.

RIDDLE-DE-DEE!

Here is a little charade to keep you on your toes. Solve the two clues to give the name of a space commander.

My first follows deadly, but comes before bad,
My second is a cream cake, that we have all had,
It's covered in chocolate, and filled with whipped cream,
Remove the first 'e' and the solution is seen.

Answer: Sinclair
(deadly sin and Sinbad
eclair - 'e' = clair)

IMPORTANT NOTICE
The Prophecy team would just like to point out that we had nothing to do with this awful poem - it's all Tony's concoction.

READER QUESTIONNAIRE.

If you are bursting with the need to congratulate our efforts, or you are seething with fury at our incompetence, or if you just have a spare five minutes, please could you fill in this questionnaire. Feel free to add any additional comments. On receipt of the questionnaire, we will send you a voucher for 50% off your next 3 issues of Prophecy. Thank you for your time.

1. How often do you buy Prophecy?
-Every month.
-Every few months.
-Very rarely.

2. How many people will share/read each copy bought?
- just one.
- two-three.
- 4+.

3. How old are those people who read it? (Tick the appropriate spaces as many times as possible e.g. 15-24 could have two ticks.)
- Upto 14 years old
- 15-24   ....
- 25-30   ....
- 30-40   ....
- 40-60   ....
- 60+   ....

4. On a scale of 1 - 5, where 5 is the highest, how do you rate our regular stories?
- Hero/Creature/Bad Guy of the month. ....
- Make-It page.   ....
- Serialised stories.   ....
- Gallery.   ....
- Archives.   ....
- Convention reviews and features   ....

5. Do you think there is a satisfactory balance between literature, film, and artwork?
Yes ....
If no, which areas should be drawn out more?
....

6. Do you think that science-fiction should form a greater or lesser part of the magazine than it does now and why?
-Greater, because ....
-Lesser, because ....
-No change   .....

7. How do you find the style of language in the magazine?
-Too formal ....
-Too casual ....
-Too lightweight ....
-Other..

8. Do you have any suggestions for future features/regulars?
....
....
....

9. Do you find there is a suitable balance between serious and cartoon artwork?
....

10. Do you find the price bearing in mind this is a monthly and has 100% full-colour printing?
-Reasonable ....
-Too expensive ....

11. Do you think that the magazine would be better as a smaller weekly than a monthly?
- Weekly ....
- Monthly ....

12. Do you think there is a satisfactory amount of involvement between the magazine and the readers via such pages as the Make-It page?
- Too much ....
- Too little ....
- good balance ....

THANK YOU

Please send your questionnaires to the normal address on the contents page.

FIG 5.5 *A reader questionnaire for* Prophecy *magazine*

What you have learnt

1 *People can take control of the media themselves, but it is not easy to sustain the effort without commercial backing.*

2 *Alternative publishers have a different approach to commercial activity, but still need to create and keep an audience.*

3 *Technology is critical to alternative publishing and high production values are difficult to achieve without the appropriate access to technology. Cost is a critical factor in this.*

4 *Alternative publishing challenges mainstream dominant representations by trying to create access for under-represented groups.*

Further thoughts

In this chapter we have used the term **access** in slightly different ways:

1 The first unit asks you to critically examine the claims made by new technologies that they give greater freedom to individuals to make a choice, i.e. they give greater access.

2 The second unit asks you to explore how, in creating more opportunities for people to buy its products, a media organisation seeks to monopolise the global market by extending its market to as many people as possible.

3 The third unit asks you to explore the way in which individuals or minority groups seek to represent viewpoints which the more commercially led media organisations ignore.

People who argue for greater representation of alternative viewpoints in the media have difficulty by definition in attracting large audiences and therefore lack capital from advertising to keep going. Some alternative media producers will not consider using advertising at all. For those that do, the advertisers have to be selling products which the editorial team approve of; this can cause a lot of problems for groups seeking to represent a particular viewpoint.

Many people believe that the mass media do not reflect the diversity of viewpoints brought about by different groups, political ideas and lifestyles. Some go further and argue that such viewpoints are deliberately excluded because they are not popular. There can be problems even when the media organisations make space for alternative viewpoints, because in general the organisations keep control of the production processes. You would not be allowed to produce a television programme for a major channel though you may well have the ideas and take part in it. Even a programme like *Video Diaries* on BBC2 is controlled by the professionals.

You might like to consider some ways in which media organisations seek to represent a variety of viewpoints:

● the use of party political broadcasts
● community access slots on radio and television
● the use of feedback programmes of viewers' and listeners' opinions
● the use of the letters page in magazines, newspapers and comics

● the use of phone ins in all the media
● balance in news reporting.

In each case it is worth thinking about the degree of control that the media organisation has over the viewpoint being expressed.

Another way of examining this issue is to consider the work of some of the organised groups who aim to influence the representations in the media. Some important ones are:

● the National Viewers' and Listeners' Association
● the Campaign for Press and Broadcasting Freedom
● the Deaf Broadcasting Council.

You could study their aims and objectives and consider how far you share such views.

2

MEDIA FORMS

Introduction

More about media language

Media language is to do with the ways in which the different media make meanings for their audiences. Each medium combines sound and visual material in different ways. The ways in which the media mix these depends, as you have seen in the first part of this book, on a complex set of relationships between the producers of media texts and the audiences they seek to create, keep and expand. In the second part of this book you are asked to concentrate on the main media in turn, focusing on the forms and genres which are covered in GCSE Media Studies. It is important that you carry forward your understandings, knowledge and skills so that your experience of the media deepens and your examination of them becomes more probing and precise.

ACTIVITY

In groups, explore how the different media of film, television, radio, comics, magazines and newspapers might deal with the issue of teenage boredom. Discuss your findings in terms of what they have in common and what makes them different.

One of the results of this activity is likely to be a need to find words to describe these differences and similarities. In Part 1 of this book you learnt some of these words: cut, shot, sound effect, *mise en scène*, narrative, genre, point of view, montage, caption, crop, sequence, anchorage, stereotype, etc. You now need to go on to explore this kind of language in a more complex way.

One important way at GCSE level is through the relationship between textual study and textual production. In this approach all media material is thought of as a text which can be read by the audience. Just as when you read a book you enjoy and understand it more if you can read the words and follow the drift, so when you experience a media text you have a much better chance of working out what the material means if you understand its language and organisation. After working through the first part of the book you should already understand that the meanings of media texts do not only depend on the organisation of the text but also on the experiences that we bring to the texts. We hope that your explorations and examination of the main media forms in Part 2 will be enriched by the knowledge and understanding you now bring to them.

Revisiting signs and conventions

The meanings of media texts are signalled to us through the combination of signs. To start your study of different kinds of media texts, you need to start with the meanings of signs.

1 What do these signs mean? How do you know? Think about the letters of the alphabet.

11 5 5 16
7 15 9 14 7

2 How many guesses do you need to complete the following sentence?
Media _____ _____ to _____
_____ media _____ and_____.

Both these examples rely primarily on a knowledge of the codes and conventions of the English language. The first relies on your knowledge of the conventions of the English alphabet and the second on your knowledge of English grammar. If you try either of them in Welsh, you will not be able to make them mean what we intended because we are not using the codes and conventions of Welsh. You may also have used lots of other information. It was probably easier if you thought about who we are and for whom we are writing. Media students have to know not only about media codes and conventions, but also about who is using them and for what purposes.

ACTIVITY

The word 'wicked' is an important code word for some groups. What would it mean if it were used:
❶ as part of the description of a pair of trainers in an advertisement on Talk Radio, UK?
❷ to describe a character in a television drama series about corruption in the church?
❸ to describe a new alcoholic lemonade?

Words are a code in media texts. You must decode the words to make sense. To decode visual language requires similar skills.

ACTIVITY

In pairs, study the visual signs shown below. What do they represent?

In your discussion, it should be apparent that some visual signs look more like what they represent than others. The ones which are closest are those like photographs. Cartoons are perhaps the next closest representation, though some of you might prefer realistic works of art like portraits. The furthest away are called symbols because they represent concepts, ideas and philosophies. A special form of visual symbols can be found in science, maths and technology.

In small groups, make a collection of visual signs. Categorise them by the degree to which they resemble reality. Make a poster to illustrate your findings.

Analysing media texts

The best way to start analysing media texts is with a series of questions:

1 What is the media form?
2 What type of media text are you dealing with?
3 What are the signs? How are they organised?
4 What are the codes and conventions?
5 Who is using them and for what purpose?

All media texts are open to a variety of interpretations. These will depend on such things as:

● the intentions of the producers in the way that they organise the texts
● the different experiences and backgrounds of the audiences.

As you continue to investigate media texts it is very important to explore both of these things. As you have seen in the first part of the book, you are very much involved. Examining the media therefore means examining our own understandings and expanding them. There would not be much point in it all if we knew all the answers already!

6

Examining the print-based media

Mainstream newspapers

We all know what a newspaper looks like because we have all seen one at some time or another. Many homes receive a newspaper on a daily basis and most people have their own particular favourite. Which paper does your family like?

Categorising newspapers

Make a list of all the newspapers that are read by members of your class and their families. Now you are going to look at the characteristics of the different papers, categorising them according to circulation, ownership and size.

Circulation

See if you can categorise the newspapers according to their circulation patterns:

● daily, morning, evening, weekly and Sunday
● national, regional and local.

Find out the circulation figure for each newspaper by using the local library. These are measured by the Audit Bureau of Circulation (ABC).

Note that circulation figures do not give a full picture of how many people read the newspapers as there are more readers than copies distributed. These figures are available from the National Readership Survey.

Ownership

Now categorise the newspapers according to who their owners and editors are. You may need to visit your school/college or local library to help you. How many of the newspapers are owned by the same person or group?

Tabloid and broadsheet

Yet another way of categorising the main daily newspapers is into two groups called tabloid and broadsheet. These terms refer to the size of paper used in the printing process: broadsheet newspapers are larger like the *Independent* or *The Guardian*, whilst tabloid newspapers are smaller in size like the *Daily Mail* and *The Sun*.

● What other papers fall into these two categories?
● What other differences are there between these two types of newspaper?

In pairs, study the layout sketches for the tabloid and broadsheet newspapers shown in Figure 6.1a and b on pages 124–5 and make a list of the differences and similarities between the two layouts. Discuss your findings with the rest of the class.

Broadsheet and tabloid newspapers are often also referred to as the quality and popular press. Tabloid newspapers tend to concentrate on more popular news, like human interest stories, whilst the broadsheet papers contain more hard news like foreign affairs and business reports. You may have identified some of these points in your earlier list on differences between the two types of newspaper.

Understanding the audience

Readers generally prefer one type of paper to another, and editors and journalists are able to build up a profile of typical readers and thus target them more directly. The most normal categorisation is based on social grade. This is a classification based on the occupation of the head of the household, and it indicates the household's spending power. The table below shows the social grades, the occupation to which they refer, and the approximate proportions of each grade in the total population:

A	Higher managerial, administrative and professional	2.7%
B	Intermediate managerial, administrative and professional	14.0%
C1	Supervisory or clerical and junior managerial, administrative and professional	26.3%
C2	Skilled manual	24.9%
D	Semi-skilled and unskilled manual	19.1%
E	Casual labourers, state pensioners and the unemployed	12.9%

Who do you think would be a typical reader for the following papers?

- *The Sun*
- *The Sunday Times*
- *The Independent*
- *The South Wales Echo*

Make a prediction and compile a reader profile for each newspaper.

When you have done this, undertake a readership survey. We suggest that you interview eight to ten people about their newspaper reading habits. You will also need to find out a bit about them but be careful, your questioning should not offend and should give you the answers you need to discover how accurate your profiling was. Questions about age (broad bands are sufficient, e.g. 15–20, 20–30, etc.), gender, occupation and hobbies would be appropriate.

So, how accurate were you? We expect that you had a very good idea of what a typical reader for a particular paper is like!

Analysing newspapers

You will need a copy of a broadsheet and a tabloid paper from the same day. Working in pairs, you are going to consider the layout, the types of stories covered and the style of language used.

Front page

Begin by making notes about the front page of each paper using the following points:

- What is the name of the paper and what does it suggest?
- How many columns does it have?
- What is the lead headline?
- What are the key words in the headline?
- What are the main points of the lead story?
- Are quotations used? Whose?

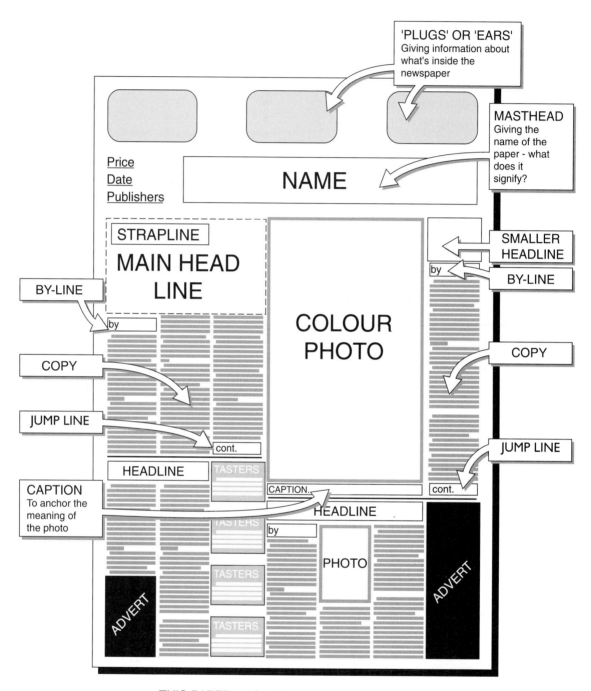

FIG 6.1 *Newspaper layouts*
(a) Broadsheet newspaper

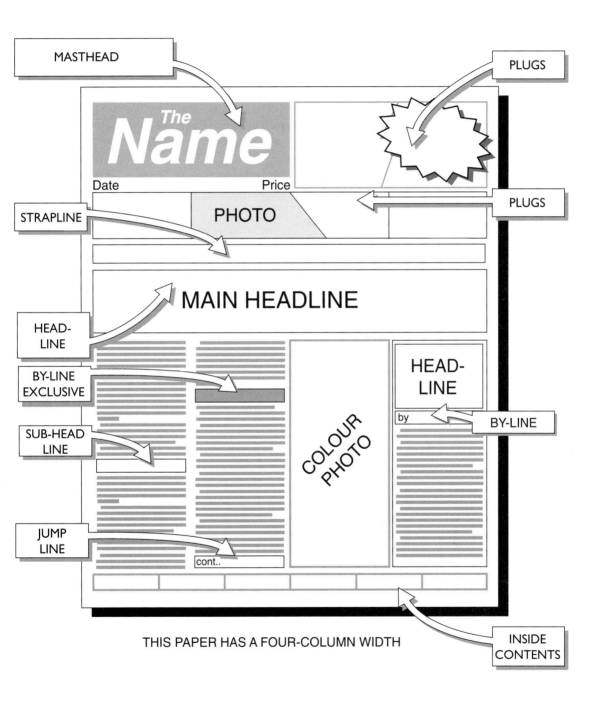

MASTHEAD

PLUGS

The **Name**

Date   Price

PLUGS

STRAPLINE

PHOTO

MAIN HEADLINE

HEAD-LINE

HEAD-LINE

BY-LINE EXCLUSIVE

by

BY-LINE

SUB-HEAD LINE

COLOUR PHOTO

JUMP LINE

cont..

THIS PAPER HAS A FOUR-COLUMN WIDTH

INSIDE CONTENTS

(b) Tabloid newspaper

- Can you distinguish between fact and opinion in the story?
- What is the main photograph?
- Has the photograph been cropped?
- Has it been used to illustrate the lead story? How?
- How does the caption anchor meaning?
- Are other photographs related to it?
- Have any been posed, or are they action photographs?

Use the same questions to look at the second story. Is there anything else noteworthy on the front page; for example, are there any adverts? What for?

When you have completed these points try to sum up, in a couple of paragraphs, the main differences between the two front pages.

Mode of address

You could also include references to the mode of address used by the newspaper. This can be determined through a study of the language used:

- impersonal or emotive?
- factual or opinionated?
- chatty or dramatic?

Does it try to involve the reader in the story by using words such as 'us' and 'our' or does it use a more formalised style of language? Are the sentences long or short? Report your findings to the rest of the class.

Inside the paper

Now look at the other pages in the two papers and make notes on the following points.

Content analysis
- How many pages cover 'home' news?
- How many pages cover 'foreign' news?
- How many pages of features are there?
- What kind of information is given?
- How many photographs are there?
- Do all the photographs accompany a story?

- How many adverts does the paper contain? For what kinds of products?
- How many pages of sports coverage are there?
- What types of sports are covered?
- How many pages of business and financial news are there?
- What other differences can you spot between the papers?
- What other similarities can you spot between the papers?

Housestyle

Every newspaper has its own housestyle and this can be determined by looking at the areas you have been studying – in particular the layout, the mode of address and the types of stories and features presented. In your group, see if you can sum up the overall housestyle of your two papers and then report back your findings, together with a target audience profile, to the rest of the class.

News values

You should have discovered by now that, depending on the newspaper, its housestyle and its target audience, certain topics and stories are more valued than others. These topics are said to contain **news value**.

News values are (unwritten) judgements that editors and journalists place upon a particular event in order to determine whether to create a story about that event. For example, royal events generally have high news value. People are interested in reading about what the royal family do and think. More 'gossipy' stories about the royals will, however, hold less value for a quality paper; they are more likely to appear in a popular paper because they are more in keeping with the paper's housestyle.

Other news values include:

- **dramatic stories:** stories with an element of

drama in them; perhaps a hijacking or a flash flood disaster

- **famous people:** stories about actors, sports personalities and politicians, particularly if they have done something wrong
- **human interest stories:** stories that feature ordinary people in difficult or life-threatening situations
- **bad news (negativity):** 'bad news is good news' so the saying goes, and newspapers rarely seem to give us good news.

Of course, stories also have to be recent and the closer they are to home (i.e. the more ethnocentric they are), the better. For example, a kidnapping in Central Africa will not feature in our newspapers unless the story also has a political or an ethnocentric value. By contrast, an event such as a kidnapping in London or Cardiff has so much news value that it is likely to appear on the front page.

Look back at your newspapers. What news values do the front pages contain?

COURSEWORK ASSIGNMENT

You have now completed enough work about newspapers to undertake a detailed comparison between two papers for your coursework folder. To organise the study, use the headings in this section as guidance.

Comics

Most of us associate comics with our childhoods.

- How many comic titles can you remember from your childhood?
- Can you draw any of the characters?
- Do you still draw comic characters?

Like a lot of other media products such as computer games, teenage magazines and cartoons, comics attract a lot of adverse criticism. Before going on with this unit, you may find it useful to review Chapter 4, which raises the question of effects of the media. This unit asks you to examine the positive claims that have been made for comics.

How to read a comic

Many people are embarrassed to be seen reading comics and yet, in fact, reading a comic is a complex business. It is clear that people who read only books find the experience of reading a comic difficult. This is because it requires a different set of decoding strategies and some readers are not familiar with them. A familiar criticism of comics is that they threaten traditional reading skills in young children. In this section you are asked to explore a comic written for young children who have to deal with diabetes. For a young child to understand this requires a great many skills that we tend to take for granted.

The frame

All comics use frames to break up the narrative. Each frame moves the narrative on in the same way as frames in film follow each other. The frames therefore represent narrative time and space.

ACTIVITY

Study the front page of *Captain B.D.A.* shown in Figure 6.2 on page 128. This is a fairly simple page, but even in this there are frames which break the normal pattern.
- Which frame goes behind the main narrative frames?
- Which frames frame break?
- Can you see why?

FIG 6.2

Frames construct the narrative by breaking time and space into unconnected moments. The reader then has to construct the connection between the frames.

The author of *Captain B.D.A.* helps the reader by using a verbal narrative to anchor the frame narrative. However, the comic can also be read using its visual language. There are a number of ways in which the author visually links the frames:

1 Look at the frame 'Then one day in the diabetic clinic he discovered an amazing power'. Explain the relationship with the next two frames. This is a **moment-to-moment relationship**.

2 Look at the frame 'With his massive fortune he built special weapons'. Explain the

relationship with the next two frames. This is an **action-to-action relationship**.

3 Now look at the frame 'He chose a name, a symbol, a costume'. Explain the relationship with the next two frames. Look especially at the use of the eyes. This is an example of a **subject-to-subject relationship**.

4 Finally, look at the opening frame. How does this link to the next four frames? In addition to the moment-to-moment relationship described above, there is a **scene-to-scene relationship**.

ACTIVITY

Take an example of a comic story which interests you.

● Count the number of frame-to-frame transitions.
● Categorise the transitions.
● Which were the most popular?

Remember that the conclusions you come to will be dependent on the type of comic you choose.

Frame management is one of the key skills of the comic writers. The shape of the individual frames is of central importance in the reading of a comic, because they contribute to the meaning of the narrative.

ACTIVITY

Read the *Captain B.D.A.* stories shown in Figure 6.3 on pages 129–31.
❶ Find a frame or frames in which time passes inside the frame.
❷ Find a sequence of frames which use similar images to stretch out a character's reaction.
❸ Study the frames which do not have borders. Can you explain why?

Time and space are not the only things which the comic writer has to represent in the frames. Sound, motion and emotions are also important.

FIG 6.3

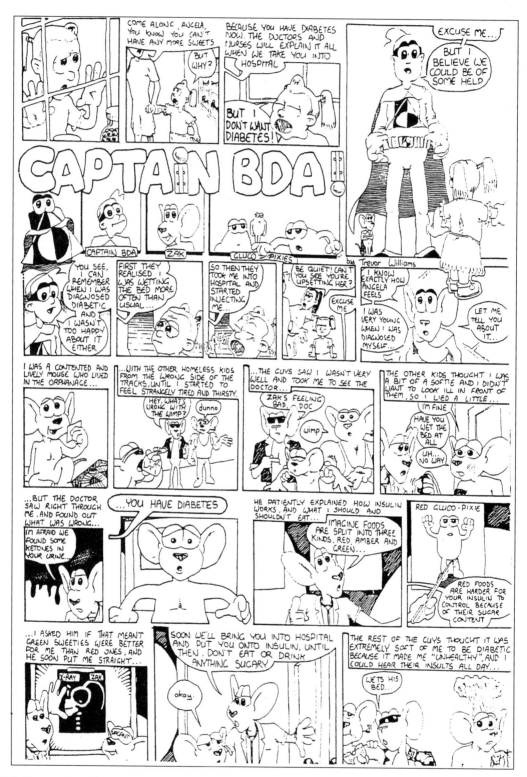

FIG 6.3 *continued*

FIG 6.3 *continued*

Representing sound

Comics contain a great deal of sound. Narrative commentary, speech and sound effects are all represented visually.

ACTIVITY

❶ **Voice-over.** Read the narrative commentary in the three *Captain B.D.A.* stories out loud. You will find that you need at least two different voices.

❷ **Speech balloons.** How many different voices can you find in the stories apart from the narrative commentary? Where do you find these voices? Are the different voices signalled by different devices? How do you know in which order to read the voices?

❸ **Sound effects.** How many different sound effects can you find in the stories? (Not all of them are words!) How many different lettering styles are there?

Representing motion

Comics also contain a great deal of movement, in addition to the movement from frame to frame. Movement is often suggested visually by **motion lines**.

ACTIVITY

Look at the *Captain B.D.A.* stories again.
❶ Find a frame in which lines suggest that a door is opening.
❷ Find a frame in which lines suggest that a character is falling.
❸ Find a frame where lines suggest that flesh is being squeezed.

Representing emotions

Comic writers are continually seeking to express emotional responses; again, they have to do this using different visual techniques.

ACTIVITY

Find frames in the *Captain B.D.A.* stories which express visually the following emotions:
● surprise
● frustration
● depression.

Shot construction

It is very useful to compare the language of film to the language of the comic, especially in terms of the construction of shots. *Captain B.D.A.* tends to use similar shots, though there are examples of close-ups and shots from different positions. Different kinds of shots, as you know from your work on film, create different meanings. So it can be useful to construct the narrative in slightly different ways to emphasise this.

ACTIVITY

Look at the beginning of the story about Angela on page 130 (the first three frames). Can you construct a point-of-view shot which will show clearly the kinds of things she longs for but cannot have?

The underlying theme of this unit is that the reading of a comic is a complex business and that, far from discouraging the development of reading skills, it actually stretches the reader as much as traditional texts. What is your opinion now?

Captain B.D.A. and the superheroes

One of the reasons that *Captain B.D.A.* works as a comic is because the writer (who was a media studies student when he produced this character) is clearly drawing on a set of narrative conventions to do with superheroes. The writer is able to draw on a set of reading skills which are drawn from the reader's experience of other media characters who have appeared in a variety of media, Batman and Superman especially.

Here are a set of conventions which could act as a working definition of a superhero:

1 He tends to be marked out from society.
2 He will have some special skills or powers.
3 He will be devoted to good causes at great personal expense.
4 He will be extraordinary in pursuing his mission in life.
5 He will need to be in disguise/costume to carry out his good works.
6 He will often have an assistant.

There are a few women superheroes, but we have stayed with the dominant tradition!

ACTIVITY

❶ Use the above list to explore the conventions of the superhero which *Captain B.D.A.* uses.
❷ Use the list to build up a table of superheroes and their characteristics.
❸ Produce your own superhero story. You could do this as a comic or, if your drawing is not up to it, you could write and produce a radio adventure. You could also parody the genre.

An international perspective on the comic form

Japanese mangas

In Great Britain comics form a very small proportion of the book market – only 1 per cent. In Japan, by contrast, comics make up 25 per cent of the book market. In other words, comics are part of mainstream Japanese culture. In Great Britain the audience for comics seems to be mainly male (between 80 and 90 per cent) and

under 30 years old. Fans in this country believe this reflects the way in which comics have been marketed in Great Britain. *Manga* is the Japanese word for comic. There are all sorts of mangas: sci-fi, teenage, sports, mahjong, gay. Manga artists have the status of pop stars and are really important figures in Japanese culture. They are style leaders for young people because they are a group who can dress and act in ways which are generally not acceptable in the conventional Japanese culture. At a comics convention in Hong Kong in 1995 with 400,000 delegates, Tezuka, a manga artist, turned up and caused a riot.

One Japanese comic genre has been of particular interest to British readers: sci-fi manga. The interest has been generated by certain animated films released in Great Britain. These are called animes; they are literally manga stories which have been animated. Two of the most famous are *Akira* and *Ghost in the Shell*. There is now a distribution network in Great Britain for both manga and anime. It has been sustained by fans who regularly subscribe to magazines, attend conventions, and purchase merchandising, videos and, of course, comics. Much of the marketing in Great Britain has been targeted at young males between the ages of 17 and 25, although it is important to stress that in Japan the appeal is much wider. In Japan, there is no sense of being ashamed to be seen reading a comic. You can tell that manga stories are not yet mainstream in Great Britain because animes have a late night/early morning slot on Channel 4. You are likely to know more if you subscribe to the new sci-fi channel from BSkyB.

ACTIVITY

GENOCYBER: A DEADLY NEW LIFEFORM UNLEASHED
This is the title and strapline of a sci-fi manga published in Britain in 1995. Study the selected pages shown in Figure 6.4 on pages 134–5. It is clearly aimed at an older audience than that which is traditionally assumed for comics.

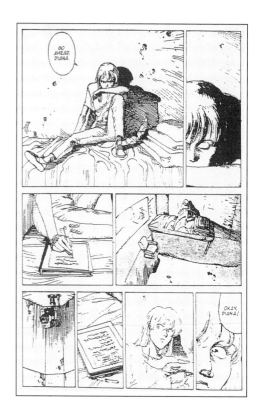

FIG 6.4 *Sample pages from* GenoCyber: A Deadly New Lifeform Unleashed

❶ The story promises the reader cyber adventure and psychic action. Can you see what these terms mean? How is this promise kept in the material?
❷ Innovative use of frames and high-quality drawing are characteristic of manga. How have the frames been used to create meaning on the sample pages?
❸ Many readers react to the portrayal of violence in this kind of manga. What issues does it raise for you?

APPLESEED SIDE STORY
Study the sample pages from a new sci-fi manga, *Manga Mania*, shown in Figure 6.5 on pages 136–8.
❶ How are the frames organised to show the reader the central character's reactions to her experiences?
❷ The manga artists are often criticised for their representation of women in that they do not look like Japanese women. This manga, for example, represents young women with very wide open eyes. What is your reaction to this?

Representation

An issue which comics raise over and over again is stereotyping. In order to visually identify characters quickly, they have to be simplified and exaggerated. Comics and animation both share this element of the cartoon. Cartoons are one of the best ways of creating viewer identification. It is why we can all remember characters from cartoons, comics and animations. This necessary simplification allows the reader to concentrate on decoding the complexities of meaning in the narrative. This is one of the reasons why readers of comics want high-quality art. Some artists are more realistic than others, but all of them use some cartoon elements. Just because there is simplification and exaggeration at one level, it does not mean that there cannot be complexity at other levels.

Mainstream magazines

Go to any newsagent's shop and you will see a wealth of magazines, which proves that there is a big market for these products. The magazine market is intensely competitive and magazines are often very specialist. Even if you do not buy magazines on a regular basis, it is unlikely that you have never glanced through one.

Over the past year we made this list of our encounters with magazines:

● read some in the doctor's and dentist's waiting rooms

FIG 6.5

FIG 6.5 *continued*

FIG 6.5 *continued*

- bought some to pass the time on a rail journey
- had some given as a present when ill
- had one given by a friend because he thought an article would be of interest
- bought some as a holiday treat to help relax.

From this we can see that magazine reading is linked in the mind with pleasure and leisure.

FIG 6.6 *Just browsing*

ACTIVITY

In small groups, discuss your encounters with magazines in the past year and make a list of your findings. Report back to the class as a whole and see if any patterns of use emerge.

Not all readers of magazines are as casual as we. Magazines depend on brand loyalty and audiences having the regular habit of buying and reading them. Magazines which do not do this do not attract advertising and so close down. So magazines make strenuous attempts to attract and keep their audiences.

There are all kinds of magazines and you have already looked at the differences between those which cater for a mainstream audience and those which cater for minority audiences in Chapter 5.

Teenage magazines

Teenage magazines are very controversial at the moment because some adults believe that they have a bad influence.

Disapproval of these magazines is mounting. Here is a list of common complaints about teenage magazines; you may be familiar with many of them!

1 The magazines are too concerned with sexual matters.

ACTIVITY

In groups, study examples of the front covers of popular magazines such as *Sugar*, *Just 17*, *Smash Hits*, *Mizz* and *More*. What age range are they aimed at in general? Can you build a profile of a typical reader?

Look at the contents pages. These will list and trail the articles. Categorise the types of articles: interviews, advice, gossip, features, fiction, real-life stories, photo-stories, etc.

2 The magazines make teenage girls too self-conscious about appearance, weight, etc.
3 The magazines encourage girls to spend too much by advertising luxury goods.
4 The magazines treat girls as though they are

interested only in boys and do not deal with issues such as ambitions, hobbies, etc.

5 The magazines encourage girls not to expect much from life.

6 The magazines encourage mindless adoration of brainless hunks.

7 The magazines feed customers to the music and fashion industries.

8 The magazines are trying to hook the readers who will later go on to read adult magazines.

9 The magazines encourage stereotypes.

10 The magazines stop students reading better material and getting on with their studies.

ACTIVITY

In pairs, decide whether you agree or disagree with the above statements. Jot down the reasons for your opinions.

Report back to the class. Emphasise the positive aspects about magazines which may counteract these arguments.

The effects of the media on society and on young people in particular are hotly debated.

ACTIVITY

Study the two pages from a local newspaper shown in Figure 6.7 on pages 141–2. How far do you find your concerns reflected in the articles?

More on media effects

In the past, it was thought that media products had a direct link to opinions and actions. This was sometimes called the 'hypodermic' effect, in which critics of the media proposed that media products were addictive in a literal sense. The media were like a drug. In more recent times it has been found that audiences are not so easily

influenced; they are not passive consumers but take an active control over their responses to media products. This approach to audiences is sometimes called the uses and gratification theory. It suggests that audiences have many reasons for making use of media products; for example, they offer:

● escapism and pleasure

● a perspective on your own identity by supplying role models, recognisable situations, shared beliefs, etc.

● a shared experience that allows you to share your thoughts on the latest soap or magazine with other media users

● educational information: facts about the wider world, varieties of experience and viewpoints, etc.

Many of these things can be positive or negative. We suggest you write a defence or mount an attack on teenage magazines using clippings and references from particular magazines as evidence.

ACTIVITY

AUDIENCE RESEARCH

In groups, conduct a survey to investigate why people like magazines. Here are some key points to help you.

❶ Target people in a specific age range or who have a specialist interest.

❷ Divide the survey instrument (the questions) into sections which explore

● knowledge (e.g. Which of the following are teenage magazines?)

● opinion (e.g. Which of the following words suggest *Just 17*?).

❸ Be clear about what you want your questions to find out (e.g. Why do teenagers read magazines? How much do boys really know about teenage magazines?).

❹ Will visual techniques (e.g. graphs/graphics/diagrams) help the presentation of your findings? For example, consider Figures 6.8–6.10 on pages 143–4: graphs produced by students investigating soaps.

Lifestyle

From Dopey Dora to sexual positions

The racier side of girls' magazines

MPs are trying to curb the sale of sexually explicit girls' magazines to young children. JULIA STUART examines what messages the publications are giving ... and why so many girls want to read them.

CONTRAST OF TIME: A February edition of More, above, and a 1973 Bunty Book of Girls, right. Notice the difference between two pages from My Guy, below right. The top one was from 1981, the lower page from an edition published this year.

PICK up a girl's magazine from less than 20 years ago and you could find tips on how to clean your antique clothes, and cartoon stories with such titles as I Remember Love.

Features in Jackie included 50 ways how to be a "winter winner":

"Top up your August tan with a sun-ray lamp and act mysteriously when they ask when you got back from Bermuda!" it gushed.

"Make the most of the snow by wrapping up messages in snowballs and throwing them at the boys you like!" it teased.

"Give up cycling to school and go by reindeer instead!" it chortled.

The comic Bunty told stories of Dopey Dora, Superstitious Cindy and the schoolgirls, the Four Marys. The annuals had pictures of dogs on the inside covers.

Sex is just a part of it

- Trevor Church, head of Swansea's Olchfa Comprehensive School, says schools are obliged by the National Curriculum to offer sex education within a health education programme.
- And all pupils attending them (parents have the right to withdraw their children) gain an adequate knowledge of sex and relationships.
- Mr Church, who has two daughters aged 11 and 13, said the danger of articles such as "position of the fortnight" is that they give youngsters a false impression about relationships and sex.
- "It gives sex a more important role in a relationship, when what we try to encourage is a warm, close and meaningful relationship" he said.
- "We try to say sex is just a part of a relationship."
- He added that he would be very unhappy if such a magazine was widely available to children under the age of 18.
- All magazines in the teenage market currently have no age restrictions and are available at newsagents.

The raciest, My Guy, included "heart-touching" romantic tales and photo love stories. The problem pages tackled such thorny issues as weak nails, blackheads, flea bites and waxy ears.

Next month's edition of Sugar, currently the most popular girls' magazine, boasts a 16-page sex special. It explains in glorious colour how to put on a condom, offers a first-hand account of abortion, and includes a "No-sex Guide to Fun", explaining how to fondle private parts.

It seems girls are no longer troubled about ear wax. The problem page tackles a warty penis, cold sore kissing,

swimming during menstruation, lumpy breasts and painful testicles through lack of sex.

Sugar says it is targeting 13 to 18-year-olds.

RIVAL More! has an article on four blindfolded women trying to guess the sexual history of a mystery bloke by snogging him.

Illustrations for other features include News of the World-type canoodling couples trying to look seductive with next to nothing on.

The two-page Sex Talk feature includes a position of the fortnight — illustrated. The publishers claim to be targeting 18 to 24-year-olds, yet the cover screams "Smart girls get more!"

The editorial content and layout is blatantly juvenile.

Marie O'Riordan's editorial leaves the reader in no doubt as to which age group she is addressing:

"Us More! girls are not known for being shy and retiring when we go on the pull so I was gagging to see how we'd compare to a bunch of lechy lads out looking for a bit of skirt action."

Bliss has a 16-page section on "boys, sex and you", My Guy's problem page advises a confused Boyzone fan on masturbation and Mizz explains with a hand-drawn picture the differences between an uncircumcised and circumcised penis.

MARKED PERSONAL

MY DREAM— HER HEARTBREAK

READERS' TRUE LIFE STORIES

RAPED AT A VALENTINE PARTY!

Articles are exactly what all the youngsters want to read

JUDGING from their sales figures these magazines are exactly what young girls want.

With a circulation of 318,000, Sugar has 130,000 more readers than the popular women's fashion magazine Vogue.

Swansea's 16-year-old triplets Katherine, Victoria and Jennifer Godfrey, regularly buy girls' magazines

for advice on growing up. All three, despite having sex education at school and at home, find the magazines very informative.

Katherine, a More! reader, describes its information on sex as very helpful.

"You really should be educated about sex from your parents mainly, and the rest you should be taught in school," she said.

"The magazines have given me a good attitude about sex."

Mizz reader Victoria feels

that More!'s sexual content is too detailed. Jennifer, a Sugar reader, is happy about the sexual content of the magazines, saying they always address contraception and how to avoid sexually transmitted diseases.

Mum Gill is concerned about the message the magazines could give to boys, who inevitably read them.

"When boys see so many articles on sex they could get the impression girls are ready and available for it. They may put more pressure on girls to have sex," she said.

Facing facts

ACCORDING to a report by Health Promotion Wales:

- Three out of four people in Wales felt inadequately informed about sexual matters when they first had sex.
- School-based sex education does not hasten the start of sexual activity.
- Fewer than five per cent of people in Wales disapprove of intercourse before marriage.
- Friends remain an important source of information about sex.
- Young people in Wales are less likely to be using contraception than those in the UK.

FIG 6.7

The page for discerning young people.

Magazines for young people have come in for some real stick lately. Today the readers have their say. Here SARAH HUMPHRIES, of Llanelli, gives her views.

Lifestyle

From Dopey Dora to sexual positions

The racier side of girls' magazines

YPs are trying to curb the sale of sexually explicit girls' magazines to young children. JULIA STUART examines what messages the publications are giving ... and why so many girls want to read them.

PICK up a girl's magazine from less than 20 years ago and you could find tips on how to clean your antique clothes, and cartoon stories with such titles as I Remember Love. Features in Jackie included 50 ways how to a "winter winner."

"Top up your August tan with a non-rip and act mysteriously when they ask you get back from Bermuda?" it said.

"Make the most of the show by wrapping messages at snowfalls and cinemas."

CONTRAST OF TIME: A February edition of More, above, and a 1973 Bunty Book of Girls, right. Notice the difference between the pages from My Guy, below right. The top one was from 1981, the lower page below published this year.

IN FOCUS: A Lifestyle feature on the fears surrounding teenage magazines.

WITH debate raging on age limits for teenage magazines isn't it about time that we, the young readers were given the opportunity to have our say?

The argument supporting a minimum age for reading teenage magazines revolves around the belief that there is too much information about sex and relationships in publications aimed at those as young as 13, and read by children as young as 10.

In cases such as this, surely it is the responsibility of the parent to monitor what the child is buying.

Magazines such as Sugar and Just Seventeen are supposedly too explicit and open about sex — some experts and parents believe that their own daughters are too young to need to know about "these things."

Information that has sent sparks flying varies from sexual positions and contraceptive options to teenage pregnancies and abortion.

Many parents believe that their teenagers should be exposed to nothing more suggestive than 10 Quick Kissing Tips.

TEENAGERS of today, however, are more aware of sex, sexuality and relationships and seem to be a great deal more mature than teenagers of 20 — even 10 — years ago.

I believe that by putting a minimum reading age on magazines, society will regress . By the time the teenagers of today have fast-maturing children of their own, sex will once again become taboo.

Denial of information on sex supplied by teenage magazines is likely to arouse curiosity and tempt teenagers into experimenting with sex, unaware of the reasons why they should be having sex, what precautions they should take and what the consequences can be.

In that case, is there any real harm in a group of teenage schoolgirls sitting in the corner of the school yard, innocently giggling over something like More magazine's Position of the Fortnight?

These articles are the only source of information that many girls (even boys), receive on sex. Sex education in a majority of schools is straightforward, scientific and out of a text book.

Parents are often mortified at the prospect of having to discuss sex with their son and daughter.

It is my belief that any girl old enough to have a child have a right to receive the information provided in teenage magazines. In any case, teenagers don't buy magazines simply to read about sex. Much material is devoted to the rich and famous, the environment, careers, hair and beauty and readers' true stories.

It seems that the people wanting to impose an age limit want to do so in order to avoid upsetting the older generation.

They fail to understand that teenage magazines are not aimed at them, but at us teenagers.

We all have the opportunity to make choices. If the adults of society find these magazines offensive, they don't have to read them.

We, as individuals, also have a choice ... and judging by the popularity of such magazines, surely the choice we have made is obvious.

They're our mags so it's OUR choice

Sex keeps on selling

"The A to Z of SEX" — a headline from a teenage magazine.

The days of Bunty are over and today's magazine publishers have got one thing going for them — sex sells. But should they be selling it to 12-year-olds?

Every girl likes to read about the things that she gets up to, but when the boundaries between fantasy and reality fade things get dangerous.

With magazines like this surely young girls get confused as to exactly what their peers borders get up to.

If a young innocent constantly reads problem pages filled with

Emma Davies sees trouble ahead thanks to magazines like More and Sugar.

readers writing in about dilemmas over certain intimacies with their boyfriends, then surely she will feel inadequate and immature.

Some say the mags help build the confidence of the reader. But I think things have got out of hand on the teeny-bopper front. I just hope that it's a phase or else I predict a serious population rise in the next decade!

It could be worse ...

SOME adults believe that our magazines are as bad as porn. But if age limits were to become law the situation would worsen. Under-age readers would find it exciting to buy copies of such publications. Even more would be purchased — shops wouldn't care whether the customer was between a certain limit.

These magazines offer educational information, readable articles along with competitions, stories and showbiz gossip. Most of these subjects are of interest to our age group.

So before adults make up their minds on these magazines, shouldn't they think what they would be like without their favourite read every week?

Cerys Pugh asks: 'Our reading matter — is it porn?'

FIG 6.7 *continued*

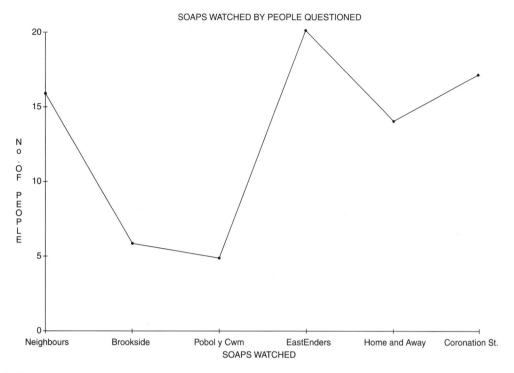

FIG 6.8

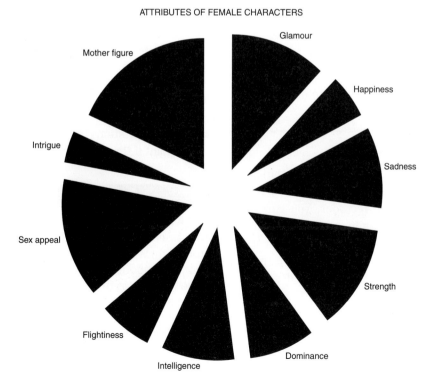

FIG 6.9

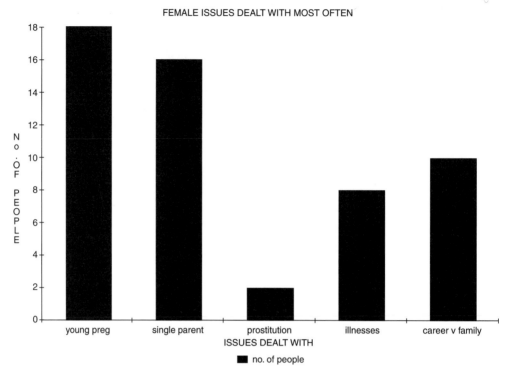

FEMALE ISSUES DEALT WITH MOST OFTEN

FIG 6.10

❺ Do not just summarise your findings, comment on them as well. Were you surprised or do they confirm your previous understandings? Do your findings have any connections with the uses and gratification theory?

Another method of obtaining information on media effects is to use **semi-structured interviews**. Use a cassette recorder. You could use the interview to gather information, or the interview could be presented as evidence of research. You could interview young people about their reading habits and attitudes to controversial material. These interviews are semistructured because you need to plan the questions carefully, but also need to be able to adapt in response to promising issues which crop up. Planned flexibility is the key. Plan your questions carefully but:

- listen to what the person is saying; pick up interesting comments and try to develop them in ways which are appropriate to the issue you are investigating
- be prepared to ask a spontaneous question if the person says something interesting to you
- use your questions to bring people back to the point if they start to ramble on.

ACTIVITY

CREATING THE AUDIENCE
Your research work will help you in your production work, since by now you must have clear ideas about what types of products young audiences like. In this activity you are going to create a magazine for a slightly different audience. Choose one of these audiences:
- young 11–13
- male teenagers
- fans
- PC teenagers.

Work in a team and give out roles to different team members:

- agony aunt
- features editor
- fashion
- film, TV, computer games, video critic
- interviews and gossip
- advertising.

Here are some key points which will help you carry out this activity.

1 Generate your own material, but do not worry if you cannot access the technology. A sense of layout and neat presentation can still produce excellent results.

2 Make use of montage, using bits of print from other sources and photographs when appropriate. Don't overdo this. Be creative in terms of design to make it lively and appealing to the target audience.

3 Test out your product using a focus group of the target audience, or by a reader questionnaire as in the earlier unit on computer games (Chapter 4). This will help you evaluate the success of your efforts as a media producer.

Examining media forms

Animated cartoons

Animated cartoons are now at the forefront of new technological advances. Sophisticated computerised paint-box systems like the quantal system allow a vast range of visual images to be constructed. Two and three dimensional computer-generated animation sequences are becoming commonplace, and the combining of computer-generated scenes with traditional film-making techniques, such as the use of live action backgrounds with cartoon characters superimposed on to them, have become popular. Animated computer games are widely played and many personal computers (PCs) have graphics packages that include cartoon characters.

The cartoon is clearly big business!

Generally cartoons tell stories; sometimes they are humorous with characters such as Goofy or Bugs Bunny, and sometimes they are action/adventure stories like *Masters of the Universe* or *Skeleton Warriors*. Longer cartoons, such as *Beauty and the Beast* and *Snow White*, use fairy tales as the basis for their plots and others, such as *Batman* or *Superman*, make links between the static animation of comics and the moving animation of the cartoon film. Some, like *The Snowman*, are aimed at a children's audience, whilst others, like Joanna Quinn's *Girl's Night Out*, are made with a more adult audience in mind. Animated sequences also appear in adverts and are juxtaposed with real characters in feature films.

So, what do they all have in common?

ACTIVITY

List the main features of a cartoon. You might like to consider characters, stories, props and locations. You will also need to consider the technical aspects of drawing and design.

The *Oxford Pocket Dictionary* defines a cartoon as 'a sequence of drawings telling a story' and 'an animated sequence of these on film'. To 'animate' something is to give life to it.

Of course, animation is a term that covers more than just the cartoon. What other forms can you list? Although this unit is concerned primarily with animated cartoons, you should also look closely at other forms of animation. Consider a short film like those starring Wallace and Gromit. Why do you think they have become so popular? At whom do you think they are targeted?

FIG 7.1 *A montage of cartoon characters drawn by students*

Realism

Obviously cartoons need to have some sense of realism in order to appear lifelike and therefore believable to the audiences that are watching them. As you have seen with comics, simplification is a central process. So cartoons often contain stereotypes which help make the characters more identifiable, use stories so that audiences can follow the action easily, and use locations and props that add to an overall sense of visual realism. In film animation or computer games, fans regularly comment on the quality of the graphics. You can study how the relationship between the characters, locations and props is based on degrees of representational realism.

Making cartoon narratives

In Chapter 1 you looked at elements of film narrative. Now you are going to develop your knowledge of narrative and use this to produce an outline for a new cartoon sequence.

Classical narratives – which most films and TV programmes adhere to – follow a linear pattern and have a beginning, a middle and an end. During the beginning section, the location and main characters are established and the plot is introduced. The middle section develops the plot and establishes an enigma: this is an area of conflict, a problem or a puzzle that the end section resolves. The classical narrative structure therefore has three parts:

1 introduction
2 enigma
3 resolution.

ACTIVITY

Analyse a short cartoon and see how it fits into the above pattern. Discuss your findings with the rest of your group.

Remember, the narration is the way in which the story is told: there are different ways for films, television programmes, comics, books and cartoons. Do not forget that news stories also have narratives, so the same story can be narrated in different ways in different newspapers. Even news programmes can have a narrative structure: a recognised way of putting the individual news stories into a sequence which the audience can follow.

For cartoons you need to consider:

● **technical codes:** drawing styles, lighting, colour, camera framing, camera angles, editing, special effects
● **representational codes:** stereotypes, settings, locations, costumes and props
● **audio codes:** music, dialogue and sound effects.

All these elements help to actually tell the story. For instance, dark colours and large gothic style buildings usually indicate a horror sequence, whilst pastel colours are more likely to indicate a softer – perhaps romantic – sequence. Certain costumes place the cartoon characters in a space or futuristic setting and others in a more contemporary setting. Dialogue, of course, gives us a great deal of information about the characters and their action in the story, and music is a good indicator of mood: orchestral for romance, discordant for tension.

ACTIVITY

MAKING A TREATMENT AND STORYBOARD
Details of a new Saturday morning cartoon series are given below:
Scheduled: Saturday morning, BBC1
Duration: 15 minutes
Title: *The Ice Warrior*
Setting: Futuristic
Give a treatment for the first three episodes and design a storyboard sequence for the first five minutes of the opening programme. Consider carefully the combination of visual signs and

technical codes you need to develop and remember to give consideration to the aspirations of your target audience. In order to find out more about your audience, you could conduct an extended interview with a small group of younger children who watch cartoons. Find out:

- which programmes they watch
- what storylines they like best
- whether they are frightened or amused by any of the action
- how real they think it is
- who their favourite characters are

- how they would imagine the Ice Warrior to look
- where they think he came from.

You could tape record your interview and use the information you have been given as the basis for your programming ideas.

To complete this work you could design some publicity material for the series and then return to your target audience group to see if it is a programme that they would like to watch. Finally, present your practical ideas, using the evidence from your pre-production work to evaluate them.

Documentary

What is a documentary? Look carefully at the word itself and see if you can come up with a workable definition for the term.

The *Oxford Pocket Dictionary* defines a documentary as something that provides a factual record or a report.

Documentary photographs

Nowadays we tend to associate the documentary with a particular genre of programmes, but its origins predate the advent of television. Photographs document events and most of us have collections of family photographs that document ourselves growing up, on our holidays or at important family functions.

ACTIVITY

Bring in a selection of photographs from home and discuss their significance to you and your family with other members of your group.

Many of these appear to be simple snaps, but

they also have a much deeper significance for the photographer and the participants.

ACTIVITY

MAKING A PHOTO-ESSAY
Working in a small group, storyboard a photo-essay about one of the following topics:
❶ **Arrival:** document the variety of ways that students arrive for school/college in the morning.
❷ **Break-time:** record how different people – staff and students – spend their break-time.
❸ **The library:** document some of the events that occur in the library during an average day.
In order to complete this task satisfactorily, you will have to begin by undertaking some research before you start on your storyboard. Ask people within the class; then make notes at the appropriate times and places.

If you have access to a camera, you could photograph your storyboard ideas and construct a classroom display. Remember, the title and photographs should provide all the information needed. No other words should be used. If you don't have access to a camera, you can still consider how you would display your photographs.

Documentary film

Early cinema tended to be a recording of actual events rather than the narrative dramas that we expect today. Early films were extremely simple in the way that they were shot (a single camera framing a single shot) and in their subject matter. One of the earliest films, shot by the Lumière brothers in 1895, was about the arrival of a train at the station. It had no sound track and no plot, yet people who saw it were extremely excited: photographs moved!

ACTIVITY

Using the ideas that you had for your photo-essay, work out how you would adapt the material so that it could be presented as a short (three to five minute) silent film that requires nothing more than in-camera editing. Again, storyboard your ideas. What changes will you have to make to the material? Why? The central issue will be the narrative structure.

If you are able to you could shoot this film, but remember to rehearse the shots in sequence, switch off the microphone, check the lighting and use a tripod to keep the camera as stable as possible.

What you have been doing so far is selecting and ordering material for a given topic: presenting through your pictures (still or moving) a representation of reality. You are trying to anchor the meaning of your production by organising the material in particular ways. You are encouraging a way of seeing.

You know from the work that has gone into the above activities that your photographs were not the result of a spontaneous click and your film is not the result of five minutes out of the classroom with a video camera. Research was undertaken, a storyboard was completed, a narrative planned, rehearsals conducted and care was taken with the final presentation. Your doc-umentary work was constructed on the basis of decisions you made!

Television documentary

So, what about television documentaries? Are they realistic programmes portraying 'things as they really are'? Or are the programmes manufactured: scripted, filmed and edited to present a particular point of view? How real are they?

Of course, documentaries cover a wide variety of topics and programmes and use a variety of different formats; it is therefore quite a difficult genre to analyse because of the differing nature of programmes within it. For example, documentaries can be subdivided into the following types:

- current affairs
- docudramas
- fly-on-the-wall (or *verité*)
- historical
- arts
- nature.

ACTIVITY

CONTENT ANALYSIS
Using a current TV listings magazine, analyse a week's output on the four main TV channels during the evening viewing hours. Classify the documentaries into different types. In order to do this you will need to read any relevant blurb thoroughly.
- Does one channel appear to favour one type of documentary more than others?
- Have you had to add more categories to the list given?
- Are you surprised by the range of topics covered?

Why are there so many documentaries on television? Are they really popular? Try looking at a TV ratings list and see if a documentary appears in the top 20 programmes. We doubt that one would do so on a regular basis! So, if they aren't popular, why are they on?

One reason may be that they are part of the public service broadcast tradition of British television: a tradition that seeks to inform and educate audiences as well as entertain them. What do you think? Is there a place in today's television schedules for programmes that are not amongst the most popular?

ACTIVITY

TEXTUAL STUDY

For this activity you need to watch a selection of extracts from a range of documentary programmes. Groups could watch different types if possible. Consider the following points and make notes on them whilst you watch:

❶ What is the programme about?

❷ What type of documentary format have the producers chosen?

❸ Is there a narrator, a voice-over or a formal presenter? How scripted does this part of the sound track appear?

❹ Has music been added? What effect does it have?

❺ What camera angles are used more than others: close-ups, pans? How are these related to the narrative?

❻ Have any of the following visual aids been used:

- archive materials
- graphics
- diagrams
- graphs
- photos
- drawings?

Remember, these would have needed preparation.

❼ What locations are used: studio or outside broadcasts? Remember, these will have been planned and researched.

❽ Are there any interviews? Are they 'live' or do you think they have been scripted and/or edited?

❾ Are reconstructions used? Remember, these are a representation of an event not the event itself. They use actors who will need to have been employed and rehearsed.

❿ Are there any special effects: time-lapse photography, animation?

Finally, think carefully about the following points:

- Where have the cameras been positioned?
- What point of view are we given?
- How has the programme been edited?
- What effect do you think that the presence of a camera and a TV crew would have on the people being filmed?
- Has the programme been given any added 'entertainment value', perhaps through the use of drama or a celebrity voice-over on a very dramatic sound track?
- Is the programme trying to persuade the viewer? Are we meant to believe one side more than the other or has the programme been evenly balanced in its treatment of the material?
- Would you have chosen to present the topic in a different way? How? Why?

What conclusions can you draw from this study? Report your findings to the rest of the class.

COURSEWORK ASSIGNMENTS

❶ How realistic do you think documentary programmes are? Refer to two or three specific programmes in your answer.

❷ Select one of the topics given below and explain how you would present it as a television documentary.

- School: the ultimate experience!
- Cold at Christmas: the plight of the elderly
- Doctor's Surgery: a day in the life of . . .
- Supporting United: a profile of the football supporter

You should consider scheduling, programme format, programme structure and target audience. Include sample storyboards, scripts and ideas for music, narration, location and visual aids as appropriate. Use these to help you evaluate your production work.

Advertising

Advertising is such a vast topic that it would be easy to fill a book just on this subject alone. So in this section you are going to look at some selected areas of advertising:

- a basic introduction to analysis
- constraints
- the work of the advertising agency.

There are many different types of advertising, from the classified columns in local newspapers through to the mini sagas of the cinema and television. How many can you list?

    Advertising is a way of communicating a message to large numbers of people simultaneously. It is a one-way form of communication because generally, like the media that the advertisers rely on, the messages are transmitted to us but we have few ways of responding to them in return. That means that we have no feedback; we cannot comment directly about the points of view that are being offered to us except by buying or not buying the product or message.

Campaigning

Advertising does not only sell us products; it is also used to sell us causes (e.g. Greenpeace, Amnesty International or Save the Children), and it is used by the government (the largest single spender on advertising) to communicate messages to us. Recent government campaigns focused on the dangers of drinking and driving and the benefits of safer sex?

A C T I V I T Y

❶ Draw up two lists, one for causes and one for government advertising. You may like to use a newspaper to help you, because this is where a lot of charities and organisations advertise. You could also monitor an evening's worth of adverts on the television and see how many government adverts there are.

❷ Find and examine two adverts which intend to make you give money to or join an organisation. Study the language that has been used within them. Remember that language is a code. Underline words and phrases that are intended to persuade you to give or to join. How does the language combine with the images to produce an overall meaning?

Product advertising

The most common form of advertising aims to sell us products. How many adverts do you think you have been exposed to today before coming to this class? Compile a list of all the adverts you can remember seeing or hearing. You might like to consider the following as possible sources for adverts:

- radio
- breakfast TV
- magazines
- 'junk' mail
- product packaging
- billboards
- advertising space at bus or train stations
- shop fronts.

Were you surprised by the number of adverts that you have encountered and can remember?

    An American researcher (Law, 1994) has estimated that the average American will have seen 350,000 adverts by the age of 18. By our calculations, that is 53 adverts a day. How many adverts will the average American have seen by the age of 80?

    Many people would argue that this does not matter at all: that adverts are just pictures and words trying to sell us a product. We can enjoy the images, but we do not have to buy the product if we do not want to. Do you agree? Or would you admit to having been influenced by advertising at some time or another?

Some researchers believe that certain groups of people are more easily influenced by advertising: teenagers, for example. They have to wear the 'right' kind of trainers, drink the 'right' kind of cola and listen to the 'right' kind of music, otherwise they will not fit in with their peers. This creates a kind of pressure: a pressure to conform, to be part of a crowd. If you buy the right products, you will be a popular member of the crowd. Do you agree with this notion?

The key questions are these:

● Do adverts contain covert (hidden) meanings?
● Do we subconsciously react to messages contained within adverts; messages that contain something other than information about the product?

● Are we part of the advertisement? Do adverts give us information about ourselves?

Examine Figure 7.2. On the surface this is simply an advert for a new type of nappy: Little Dears. But the picture of a doting mother, and the text about how a mother can avoid hurting her baby, combine to give us a symbol of motherly love: the new nappy. The nappy itself, as a sign, becomes synonymous with care and affection. These are feelings which we experience as natural for good mothers and so the advert plays on the subconscious. The logical conclusion is that, if you do not provide this nappy for your baby, you are a bad mother because your baby will suffer! Obviously, this is a very exaggerated example of the manipulative nature of adverts. It is based on an underlying threat.

AVOID THE HURT, AVOID THE TEARS LISTEN TO OTHER MOTHERS' CHEERS

AND CLOTHE YOUR BABY IN

'LITTLE DEARS'

'LITTLE DEARS' : FOR A HAPPY, DRY BABY AND A LOVING, CARING MOTHER.

FIG 7.2

Print-based advertising

In pairs, make a collection of print-based advertisements. Then divide your collection into adverts which are simply selling a product and those which are using a more complex strategy and selling us a way of life or a set of values together with the product.

What conclusions can you draw from your collection? Discuss your adverts with another pair, commenting particularly on the language that has been used. What effect do you think the advertising blurb may have on the target audience?

Analysing print-based adverts is one of the more common tasks in media studies and one that you may encounter in your final written paper. It is useful to be able to deconstruct the advert and from your deconstruction comment on the overt and covert meanings within the text, so here is a formula to help you.

When studying adverts it is useful to look at three main areas:

- how it has been made up: **construction**
- what it is about: **message**
- who it is aimed at: **audience**.

Construction

Examine the entire advert. Make a note of everything that you can see and comment on the general layout. Include notes on:

The images
- What and who is being represented?
- Have stereotypes been used?
- What is in the background and the foreground?
- Where is the advert set?
- What are the predominant colours?

Of course, for all these questions you will also need to supply the answer to the next question: why?

The text or dialogue
- How is the product mentioned?
- What part does it play in the advert itself?
- Is the language used emotive, persuasive or factual?

The narrative structure
- Do the images and text combine to tell a story?
- Is it relevant to the product?
- What do you think that particular narrative has been used to sell that particular product?

Message

What are the overt and covert meanings contained within your advert? Here you will need to comment on the implicit messages that lie behind the constructed elements.

Perhaps the product is promoting something that you cannot live without or something that will improve the quality of your life (will it really?). Or perhaps it is trying to project an image of beauty, wealth, health or happiness that will encourage you to buy the product in the hope of obtaining one of these, or at least letting other people see you have these attributes because you have the product!

Target audience

Who is the target audience for the advert? You can formulate your answer by considering the following points:

- Where was the advert positioned? There are different relationships between words and images according to which medium (newspapers, magazines, billboards, comics) you find the advert in.
- What types of people are in the advert?
- What kind of language has been used?
- What product is being advertised?

The target audience is not always obvious. Be careful that you do not generalise too much: for instance 'men' is far too broad an answer. Business men, men with families, one of the lads or pensioner may help you to narrow the audience down further, but do not fall into the trap of stereotyping groups of people in the same way that advertisers do!

In general, remember that all the elements have been constructed in a particular way to persuade the audience to purchase the product; everything within the advert is there for a reason and every sentence has been carefully constructed for maximum effect. Adverts are amongst the most intentional of media products because they clearly aim to persuade you to change your behaviour in some way.

ACTIVITY

Select two contrasting adverts from any medium and explain how the elements within each have been constructed to encourage the target audience to purchase the product. Which do you think is the more successful and why?

Advertising control

As well as attempting to inform and persuade, adverts must also be legal, honest, decent and truthful.

Whilst there are some laws which cover advertising, such as the Trades Descriptions Act, advertising in Britain is mostly self-regulated. That means that the media industries have the responsibility for regulating advertisements themselves.

In order to establish guidelines, codes of practice have been drawn up that advertisers should adhere to. Do note the use of the words *guidelines* and *should*. The guidelines are not statutory. You can get a summary of these codes

of practice by writing to the following organisations:

The Advertising Standards Authority: 2–16 Torrington Place, London WC1E 7HN.

The Independent Television Commission: 33 Foley Street, London W1P 7LB. Or check your phone book for your regional office.

The Independent Radio Authority: 14 Great Queen Street, London WC2B 5DG.

Your school, college or local library may also have copies of the codes of practice.

ACTIVITY

Working in small groups, find out what the codes say about one of the following. Distribute the topics evenly amongst the class:
- tobacco advertising
- violence and anti-social behaviour
- product placement
- advertising to children.

Present your findings to the rest of the class. Illustrate your presentation with reference to actual adverts.

Behind the image

Once a company or organisation has decided that a particular product or message needs advertising, a campaign gets underway. Obviously this needs careful and thorough planning and a company will generally approach an advertising agency which specialises in creating, producing and disseminating campaigns.

Market research will be carried out first to establish an audience for the product (or service). This may be decided by a demographic study, i.e. according to gender, race, age, occupational social class, geography or a combination of all these aspects.

Then the different departments of the agency

will meet to decide upon the right marketing mix for the product. Basically this has come to mean identifying and working on four separate areas which have become known as the four Ps: product, price, place and promotion.

Product   This includes not only creating the right product for the right audience, but also ideas about brand name, packaging and after-sales service.

Price   Of course, the price has to be right and advertising/marketing costs will also have to be taken into consideration when price fixing. Price can also be an advertising tool – offering your product at a cheaper price than a competitor. Think about the sales adverts on television: the price is always mentioned along with words such as 'quick', 'hurry' and 'bargain'. What other kinds of adverts regularly refer to price?

Place   This refers to the distribution of the product. It needs to be distributed and then prominently displayed in retail outlets that are suitable for the designated target audience. There also has to be enough of the product available. Stories abound in advertising circles of campaigns which have been more successful than the manufacturer had hoped for – to the extent that there were not enough products available for the people who wanted to purchase them!

Check out your local newsagents or corner shop and see how sweets, crisps and cans of drink are displayed. Which brand names have the front-of-the-counter spot? Are they presented in their own display unit? Retailers are often under pressure to display certain products (usually from larger manufacturers) more prominently than others.

Promotion   This area includes public relations, exhibitions, gifts, personal selling (perhaps by telephone or by people knocking at the door), as well as the more obvious aspects of advertising with which we are all familiar and you listed earlier in this section.

It is then the turn of the production department to realise the ideas and to produce the designs, packaging and materials for the advertising campaign. The media department selects the appropriate advertising medium to reach the desired target audience and negotiates with media institutions to buy space at favourable rates.

ACTIVITY

THE ADVERTISING CAMPAIGN: A SIMULATION

Working in a small group, you are going to assume the role of an advertising agency. You have been presented with a brief by your clients Better Foods Limited, a well-established company, and have been asked to come up with the details for a campaign.

Brief

Your task is to devise an advertising campaign for a new breakfast cereal. The product is made of wheat, coloured green and in the shape of tiny spaceships. It does contain food colourings (harmless), but it is low in calories and contains some fibre.

Method

After conducting some market research, you need to decide upon the four Ps, making certain that you include justifications for the following:
- a name
- price
- packaging details
- retail outlets
- the advertising.

You then need to decide upon the most effective medium/media for your campaign:
- magazines
- posters
- radio
- television
- cinema.

Your campaign may also include free offers, and models, games or T-shirts may be made available to consumers to help promote the product.

Once the details of the campaign have been decided on, you will need to construct it.

Remember the elements that you analysed when doing your deconstructions and think carefully about the images and text you want to include in your adverts. You will need to produce designs for print-based advertisements, storyboards for television or cinema adverts and scripts for radio.

End products

To complete this activity fully, you should provide the following:

❶ details of your market research and justifications for your choice of target audience (do remember that although this is a product that will appeal to small children, it is generally adults that make the purchases)

❷ a mock-up and explanation of the packaging for the product

❸ details, designs, scripts and storyboards for the advertising campaign, together with explanations of your design details and reasons for your choice of advertising media

❹ conclusions/evaluation.

It is very important that each member of the group keeps a record of the contribution he or she has made to the assignment.

8

Examining media genres

Law and order shows

Crime is currently one of the most popular genres on TV. If you are a regular TV watcher, you will know that it is difficult to escape the endless succession of police and detective dramas, reconstructed crime programmes, and documentaries highlighting episodes of illegal behaviour or 'everyday' police work.

This programme genre has been popular for many years, but much has changed since the early days of *Dixon of Dock Green* and *Z Cars*, and many different aspects of police work are now shown.

ACTIVITY

CONTENT ANALYSIS

In pairs, look in a recent TV listings magazine and see if you can log all the crime programmes currently being shown. You may like to list programmes according to channel, time-band and country of origin, and to classify the programmes according to type: drama, documentary or reconstruction. Discuss your findings with the rest of the class.

- Which do you think would be the most popular programmes? See if you can check your predictions with a recent ratings chart.
- Why do you think these particular crime programmes are popular?
- Who do you think would be the specific target audience for them? Check the listings to see where they generally occur in the schedule.

ACTIVITY

INVESTIGATION USING SEMI-STRUCTURED INTERVIEWS

Ask a sample of people what their current favourite crime drama is and also what their past favourite has been. You may need to give them a list of past programmes. Titles such as *Dixon of Dock Green*, *Z Cars*, *Softly, Softly*, *Special Branch*, *Juliet Bravo*, *The Gentle Touch*, *The Professionals*, *The Sweeney*, *Starsky and Hutch*, *Cagney and Lacey*, *Kojak*, *Hooperman*, *Bergerac*, *Columbo*, and *Miami Vice* could be included to jog people's memories. You will need to ask a range of people of different ages (we think that about 12–15 should be enough) and to devise a way of recording your answers.

When you have done this task, compare your findings with your own predictions of the types of people who watch particular current programmes. How accurate were you? How wrong were you?

Can you now compile a profile of a probable viewer for any of the programmes on the current

FIG 8.1 *Can you name the programmes that these characters appear in?*

list? Discuss your ideas with your partner and then feed back your ideas to the rest of the class.

INVESTIGATION USING AN IN-DEPTH INTERVIEW

Now we want you to compile a programme profile for one of the programmes that has been identified in your survey as a past favourite. In order to do this you will need to interview one of the people who answered your previous survey.

Think carefully about the questions that you will ask. You need to find out as much as possible about the programme. For example, when was it on? At what time? On what channel? How long was it on for? Who starred in it? What were the names of the main characters? What kinds of crimes were solved? Did the police work alone or as part of a team? Why was it enjoyable?

Rehearse your questions carefully with your partner: he or she could answer them using a current favourite and then you will be able to identify any weaknesses with your questions.

If you can, it would be a good idea to take a tape recorder along with you when you conduct your interview. A recording is much better than trying to remember exactly what people have said.

When you have collected all the information you need, see if you can find any pictures relevant to the programme. Ask your teacher or visit the library. Then write up your profile and present your findings to the rest of the class. They could then form part of a class display on 'Past Crime Times' or be kept in your folder to form part of a crime drama dossier.

- Why do you think TV companies make so many crime programmes?
- Why do you think they are so popular with viewers?

The answers to the two questions may be linked. Perhaps because there are so many crime dramas around, people are forced into watching them because there is nothing else on. Then, perhaps because people watch them, the TV companies think they are very popular!

A little too simplified, perhaps. But what other answers can you come up with? It may help you to decide this point if we now look closely at what, exactly, makes a programme part of the crime drama genre.

Conventions

We are going to explore the elements that most programmes have in common. As you read through the list, see if you can relate the points made to programmes that you are familiar with.

Narrative structures

Crime dramas tend to have predictable narratives. We know that a crime will be committed and that, usually, by the end of the programme or the serial the police will have solved it. But what other features are common to crime narratives? Look at the list below. Which bits do you agree with and which would you change? Can you add to it?

1 The police tend to work in teams or with partners. There is a bond between them and their (sometimes frank) discussions help us to interpret parts of the story we do not see.
2 The senior detective on the team often does not 'get on' with his or her boss: this can lead to problems in the solving of the crime – delays, perhaps. Battles and conflicts between different parts of the police organisation are often referred to as patch wars.
3 Conflicts often exist between the home and work lives of the leading characters and a subsidiary story relating to the personal life of one of the team may be developing within the traditional narrative framework. It may or may not have a direct bearing on the outcome of the programme.
4 We, the audience, are often presented with a range of clues that leads us to suspect the wrong person: the classic red herring ploy.
5 The audience often sees events from only one

point of view, usually the detective's, but even then the character often has a quiet, almost secretive side and all is not always revealed to us. Part of the narrative remains hidden and we are invited to take an active part in solving the crime.

Representations

Who are the 'goodies' and the 'baddies'? How can you tell simply from watching who the detectives and who the criminals are? What stereotypes are used?

ACTIVITY

In small groups, compile a brief profile for a detective for a new crime drama called *Tasker*.

Now compile a brief profile for the criminal who will appear in the first programme: a jewel thief who (we assume) murders a wealthy widow whilst undertaking a burglary at her stately home.

Discuss your profiles with the rest of the class and see if you can make a list of the common characteristics that you have identified. Our guess is that there will be a lot, because we have all become highly adept at recognising character types.

Think about the character types that rarely feature as either detectives or criminals. Why is this? Discuss with a partner reasons why certain types do not appear and then report back to the rest of the class.

Visual compositions and conventions

In crime dramas the same objects, places, dress and even decor tend to recur:

- Guns, computers and portable radios and telephones feature frequently.
- Male detectives dress in standard suits, white shirts and ties. (If the lead character does not, then a statement is generally being made about his character!)

- Programmes tend to be set in distinct locations, although 'crime scene rooms', often temporary, all look the same: desks, chairs, telephones, filing cabinets and a large pin board full of photos, maps and written details which are highly significant but never fully explained. They all appear as if by magic.

Typical narrative structures, character representations and visual conventions all combine to give us the genre identifiers and help us to read the programme we are watching.

What other elements can you identify as being typical of the genre? What about specific camera techniques such as short sequences of shots rapidly edited during a chase scene; close-up shots of guns or startled faces; or aerial shots of the criminal's house? Do different programmes have different visual styles? Can you think of any others?

ACTIVITY

OPENING SEQUENCES
Your teacher will now show you the opening sequences from a variety of crime dramas. Note the following details for each one:

Title: what does this tell you about the programme?

Graphics: how has the title sequence been constructed? Comment on its style.

Music: how does the music fit the action, pace and style of the programme? Is there anything about the music that helps you to interpret the mood of a particular scene?

Characters: what characters have you been introduced to? Can you identify the 'good' and the 'bad' characters? How?

Narrative: what predictions can you make about the plot? What do you think will be the likely outcome of the programme?

Visual conventions and compositions: what other specific features can you highlight which tell you that this is a crime drama?

Discuss your notes with a partner. Which programme do you think you would want to watch? Which programme do you think your parents would prefer to watch?

ACTIVITY

CRIME DRAMAS: DECIDING THE FUTURE
Your group represents an independent film company which has been approached by the BBC.

Brief
Your task is to present a treatment for a new crime drama. The programme will be scheduled for eight o'clock on a Friday evening and will run, initially, for five weeks. You will need to draw upon your knowledge of conventional narratives and stereotypes and, although you are free to break with the more traditional elements of the genre, your programme needs to be identifiable to your target audience.

Method
❶ Decide on:
- **the main characters:** compile detailed profiles for them
- **the main locations for your series:** describe and justify
- **the name for your programme:** it needs to be relevant.

❷ Bearing in mind your probable target audience and your given time slot, outline briefly the main narratives of the five episodes. Include any narrative strands that will run through each of the programmes.

❸ Script and storyboard the opening sequence for your first episode. This will need to include a title sequence as well.

❹ Devise some publicity material for your programme. This could include a storyboard for a trailer, an article for a TV listings magazines, or an advert for a newspaper.

❺ Individually, write a report to accompany the group's treatment. In it you should explain the choices that have been made and your individual role in the production, and give an overall evaluation of the work.

❻ As a group, sell your idea to the rest of the class.

Science fiction

The literary background

Science fiction is a film and television genre, but it started as a literary genre and those roots have had a strong influence on the way science fiction has developed. Many science fiction films started off as novels and short stories. Many TV series end up in book or comic book form. The film *Star Wars* is a good example.

Radio has also been an important medium for science fiction. A trip to any of the science fiction book shops which are springing up under such names as Forbidden Planet or Galaxy will soon reveal how science fiction is a genre which crosses the different media. The genre also has strong connections with other genres such as fantasy and horror.

Mary Shelley wrote her novel *Frankenstein* in 1816. Her creation – so often filmed, drawn and written about – raises some of the central issues of science fiction. At the end of the novel, Frankenstein's monster shouts out that he started out with good intentions and feelings but has been degraded and brutalised by the world. This regret, a feeling that science has gone too far, is a central and repeated motif of this genre.

- Can you draw the monster?
- If you can, do you know which film version you are basing your drawing on?

One of the first acknowledged science fiction writers was Jules Verne, who tended to write about marvellous machines and inventions or fabulous journeys. Jules Verne is the favourite writer of Doc in *Back to the Future 3*. Verne wrote in the middle and late nineteenth century and many of his novels have been filmed: *Rocket to the Moon*, *Voyage to the Bottom of the Sea*, *20,000 Leagues under the Sea*. He lacked, though, the insight of the later writer H. G. Wells, who was able to deal with relationships, society and politics through scientific issues. Wells also had many books filmed: *First Men on the Moon*, *The Invisible Man*, *War of the Worlds*. Wells thought that men would have difficulty in controlling science and his view of the future was bleak. Modern science fiction writers like Asimov, Aldiss, Ballard, Dick and Crichton are all powerful sources for new film projects.

ACTIVITY

SUBJECT MATTER

❶ Write down the word science in the middle of a page and make a spider diagram of what science means to you. Here are a few ideas to get you started: genetic engineering, cybernetics, psychology.

❷ In pairs, make a list of TV programmes and films which fit into the science fiction category. How did you decide? Were any very difficult to agree about? To decide you will have to discuss repeated patterns.

Genre characteristics

Typical characters

In small groups, list some typical characters of science fiction films, using these headings:

- heroes
- female roles
- villains
- stock characters.

The alien is one of the characters who is likely to have cropped up. Aliens come in many shapes and forms. Sometimes as with Mr Spock, probably the most famous alien of all time, the alien is the hero – although this was not expected when *Star Trek* was first planned. Aliens can have central roles or just give atmosphere to a place, as in the bar scene in *Star Wars*, or they can be extremely frightening as in *The X Files*.

Here are some dictionary definitions of the word alien:

1 belonging to another country
2 not natural, repugnant
3 foreigner
4 an outsider
5 in science fiction, a being from another world.

At first sight it may seem that the final meaning only is relevant, but in fact all the meanings are useful.

In the 1950s, Hollywood made a series of science fiction films, such as *Invasion of the Body Snatchers*, which used aliens as a symbol for the threat (as they saw it) of the spread of communism from the USSR. In the 1980s some critics have said that aliens in films like *Aliens* have had parallels with the threat of AIDS. This suggests that aliens can take on the characteristics of our fears, anxieties and worries.

With this complicated idea in mind, try the following activity.

ACTIVITY

❶ Design an alien for a science fiction programme of your choice. Provide concept sketches for appearance and costume. Suggest possible materials. Make a profile of the alien's character and explain how the alien would fit into a particular episode. Think about whether the alien would disappear in a single episode or whether the alien has the potential to be a recurring item as, for instance, the Klingons or the Daleks. Does your alien have a symbolic role? If so, what are the signs in your representation which the audience can read?

2 If you have access to stage make-up, make over a friend into an alien. See if you can produce a costume for the alien. Take some photographs to illustrate your ideas. Try to explain the importance of each element of the representation to your class.

Typical situations

Science fiction is a very broad term and in order to discover more about the range, look at the list below and see if you can name a film or TV programme which uses this plot:

1 Because of greed or negligence, a machine goes out of control.
2 A journey into space.
3 An unknown enemy stalks people.
4 Space aliens visit the earth.
5 World of the future.
6 Aliens or machines are found to be better than human beings.

ACTIVITY

In pairs, think of an idea for a new science fiction film. Present your initial ideas to your class to test out their reactions and suggestions. Now give a more detailed treatment suggesting locations and plot details. Small groups could concentrate on different aspects of the treatment. Make suggestions for each of the following headings:
  - basic idea
  - detailed plot (opening situation, enigma, resolution)
  - character profiles
  - locations
  - special effects.

Typical iconography

We can usually spot which genre we are watching on TV even when we are channel hopping. The visual appearance gives the genre away.

ACTIVITY

Examine the opening credits and five minutes of any space series such as *Star Trek, Babylon 5, Space Precinct*. Make a list of the objects, music, sets, costumes and gadgets which appear. If different groups are able to view different programmes, you will have a wide range of visual styles to compare.

What effect does the visual style have on the story and its atmosphere? Each group could introduce their clips and illustrate their findings.

Examining tests: a case study of *Jurassic Park*

Jurassic Park was adapted from the novel by Michael Crichton, many of whose books have been adapted for the screen: *Westworld, Coma* and the sequel to *Jurassic Park*. As a writer he tends to deal with the so-called soft sciences like biology, psychology and increasingly computer science. Nonetheless, the issues he raises are firmly established in the science fiction genre. He is particularly concerned with the question of whether we can keep control over the discoveries and inventions we make.

ACTIVITY

IS IT SCIENCE FICTION?
Make notes on typical characters, situations and iconography in the film *Jurassic Park*. Now make a case for the film as an example of science fiction.

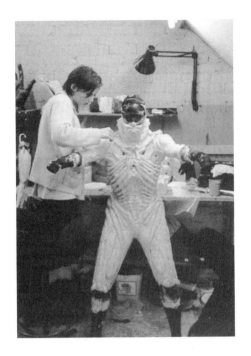

a

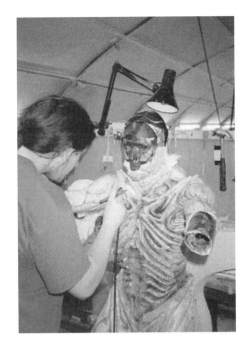

b

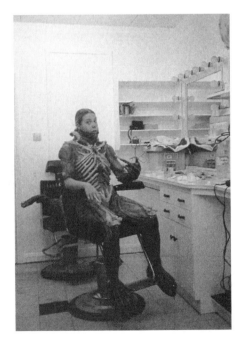

c   d

FIG 8.2 *Creating an alien is a slow, painstaking business. Actors often spend hours being*
fitted into complex suits and make-up
(a) Seaming the raw foam bodysuit
(b) Airbrushing the bodysuit
(c) The last few poppers being sewn into the joins
(d) Relaxing between takes

FIG 8.3 *This cover creates icons which are concerned with special effects of all kinds*

CLOSE EXAMINATION OF KEY SCENES

Examine two key scenes in *Jurassic Park* by viewing them several times. Make notes on the roles of characters, creation of atmosphere and science fiction characteristics. Then carry out the following tasks:

❶ Prepare a talk using shot analysis of short sequences to illustrate your findings.

❷ Read the opening section of the novel which was not used in the film. Use your notes to write a storyboard for this bit; try to use some of the techniques you noted.

❸ Choose some other scenes from the novel. Draw settings for the scenes. Make some costume sketches for the characters. Plan hairstyles for the characters.

COURSEWORK ASSIGNMENTS

This section has many suitable coursework pieces. Here are a few more you may be interested in trying:

❶ Produce a science fiction programme for radio: theme music, opening sequence; proposed treatment; a few minutes from an episode using appropriate voices and sound effects.

❷ Produce a science fiction fanzine for a favourite series.

❸ Produce a radio programme from outer space.

❹ Investigate the popularity of science fiction films.

❺ Build and photograph your own models, gadgets and characters.

❻ Plan your ideal schedule for the science fiction channel on BSkyB.

Be inventive in your own way. Be creative in your own way. And may the force be with you!

Television drama

Television drama is a huge area which covers everything from a soap opera, like *Coronation Street*, to a classic serial, like *Pride and Prejudice*. The defining features of the genre are characters and narrative. However, although drama on television can be classified as a genre in its own right, it is also made up of a series of sub-genres. When television was developing during the 1950s it was in competition with cinema. As a consequence TV chose to copy the radio formats such as crime stories and situation comedies and theatre formats with their one-off plays, rather than trying to compete with Hollywood. Ironically in the 1990s film companies have begun to copy the successful formats of the television drama with such films as *Mission Impossible* and *The Prisoner*. The many different forms of television drama illustrate television's ability to draw on a wide range of sources. In Britain there is a strong literary tradition where public broadcasting has made it a priority to bring great works of theatre and adapted fiction to the screen.

ACTIVITY

EXAMINING TEXTS

❶ Working in small groups, make a list of the drama programmes that you have watched in the past week and discuss the similarities and differences. Some key areas you may discuss could be:

● genre
● the differences between a series and a serial
● how much you liked them.

❷ Look at the typical drama programmes shown in Figure 8.4; they were all on television during the same week period. From their descriptions and your own media knowledge decide:

DRAMA
Casualty

8.05pm BBC1

Two road accidents with very different consequences in this week's episode. One involves a lad on a young offenders scheme who steals a car so that he can get away from his repressive father. No prizes for guessing that he crashes, but, not surprisingly, he is terrified of being taken to Holby City Hospital in case he is identified as the driver of the stolen vehicle. The twist in this storyline is the identity of the young man's father.

The other story is about jealousy. Convinced that her fiancé is having an affair, a young woman waits outside the hotel where he works only to see him and "the other woman" together. Enraged she drives off and, yes, she crashes too, but was she right to be suspicious about her fiance?

DRAMA
Catherine Cookson's The Girl

9.00pm ITV

Only weeks after Catherine Cookson's period drama *The Tide of Life* attracted audiences of 12 million plus, ITV is screening *The Girl*, another adaptation of one of her books.

It has a different feel to *The Tide of Life* – set in the 1860s rather than turn of the century, and tells the story of Hannah Boyle (Siobhan Flynn) who is different things to different people. To Matthew Thornton she's a beloved daughter but to his wife she is merely "the girl", a bitterly resented reminder of her husband's infidelity. Cookson herself was illegitimate, something that was a constant factor in her life and a subject frequently returned to in her writing.

DRAMA
ER

10.00pm C4

After last week's clash, handsome Dr Doug Ross (George Clooney) is after a new job in the private sector and it looks like he's got one: "Ninety grand a year and nobody dies – hallelujah and auf wiedersehen!" he announces to his colleagues.

And if viewers are going into shock at that possibility, tonight's episode offers no let up with a "999 meets *ER*" plot guaranteed to get pulses racing. George Clooney goes under the *Spotlight* on page 9.

5.20pm New Baywatch

Bash at the Beach. Wrestler Hulk Hogan and the *Baywatch* lifeguards team up to stop a youth centre being closed and turned into apartments. Meanwhile, Stephanie receives alarming news from her doctor.

Mitch Buchannon	DAVID HASSELHOFF
CJ Parker	PAMELA ANDERSON
Stephanie Holden	ALEXANDRA PAUL
Caroline Holden	YASMINE BLEETH
Cody Madison	DAVID CHOKACHI
Terry "Hulk" Hogan	HIMSELF
"Macho Man" Randy Savage	HIMSELF
"Nature Boy" Ric Flair	HIMSELF
"The Taskmaster" Kevin Sullivan	HIMSELF
Big Van Vader	HIMSELF

Stereo Subtitled 7581313

DRAMA
Black Hearts in Battersea

5.15pm BBC1

Poor Simon has had a rough time over the last five weeks. In the final part of Joan Aiken's 19th-century saga, it looks as if he's finally going to get his just deserts. Rescued from the conspirators' ship by Dido, he heads for the Duke of Battersea's country residence, where his true identity is finally revealed. But there's a long way to go before anybody can start thinking about living happily ever after.

DRAMA
Ballykissangel

7.30pm BBC1

Father Peter Clifford, an idealistic English priest, turns up in the Irish town of Ballykissangel to begin a new ministry one wet afternoon. He is not welcomed with open arms: "One thing this country needs," says sarcastic pub landlady Assumpta (Dervla Kirwan from *Goodnight Sweetheart*) "is priests from England."

Father Peter's struggles to find his feet form the substance of this six-part drama with comic touches written by Kieran Prendiville. Stephen Tompkinson plays Peter, and there's strong support from Tony Doyle as conniving businessman Brian Quigley. The series was filmed in County Wicklow, and the rain-soaked countryside plays a starring role.

8.00pm Suspicious circumstances: nothing seems quite right to Hastings (Hugh Fraser) and Poirot (David Suchet)

8.00 Agatha Christie's Poirot

CHOICE A new feature-length story about the Belgian detective. Starring **David Suchet** *Murder on the Links.* Soon after Poirot and Hastings arrive in France for a well-earned break their help is sought by Paul Renauld, who believes he is being defrauded. By the following day, Renauld is dead. **See today's choices.**

Hercule Poirot	DAVID SUCHET
Hastings	HUGH FRASER
Giraud	BILL MOODY
Paul Renauld	DAMIEN THOMAS
Bella Duveen	JACINTA MULCAHY
Lucien Bex	BERNARD LATHAM
Jack Renauld	BEN PULLEN
Eloise Renauld	DIANE FLETCHER
Stonor	TERENCE BEESLEY
Marthe Daubreuil	SOPHIE LINFIELD
Jeanne Beroldy/Bernadette Daubreuil	KATE FAHY
Loonie	HENRIETTA VOIGTS
Dr Hautet	ANDREW MELVILLE
Golfer 1	TIM BERRINGTON
Golfer 2	HOWARD LEE
Adam Letts	JAMES VAUGHAN
Dubbing secretary	BELINDA STEWART WILSON
Projectionist	SIMON HOLMES
Voice-over artist	RICHARD BEBB
Policeman 1	CHRISTOPHER HAMMOND
Policeman 2	JOSEPH MORTON
Guard	RAY GATENBY
Manager	BRIAN ELLIS
Concierge	MARGARET CLIFTON
Judge	RANDAL HERLEY
Lawyer	PETER YAPP
Tramp	TERRY RAVEN

Adapted by Anthony Horowitz
Producer Brian Eastman; Director Andrew Grieve
Stereo Subtitled 5695

DRAMA
EastEnders

7.30pm BBC1

Ricky Butcher (Sid Owen) is obviously just a boy who can't say no. He nearly scuppered his relationship with Bianca (Patsy Palmer) once before by dallying with her best friend, Natalie. Now history is repeating itself. Since ex-wife Sam (Danniella Westbrook) started turning on the charm, Ricky has once again been unable to choose between two women.

Things finally came to a head in last night's episode with an embarrassing scene that will be hard to forget. Tonight Bianca shows just what a fiery redhead she can be – but one can't help thinking that this particular love triangle isn't over yet.

FIG 8.4

- what genre the programmes represent
- what audience they would attract.

You may like to take this further by asking a range of people from different age groups which of these programmes they prefer and why. You could then write a short profile of the programme's target audience.

Trailers

Television channels vie with each other for audiences. For the commercial channels the ratings figures help to entice advertisers; for the BBC the ratings help to justify the licence fee. For the programme producers the ratings are life and death. Good figures ensure another series, poor figures mean that we will not see that programme on our screens again. A good audience is therefore essential. Audiences are targeted in a number of different ways: through the TV listings magazines; through articles in magazines and newspapers; and through trailers on television.

Trailers for a new drama series generally begin to appear on our screens two to three weeks before transmission; trailers for an established drama generally appear within a week of transmission. All have the same function: to raise our expectations so that we will watch the programme.

In order to do this a trailer has to contain several elements. In addition to giving us the name of the programme it must:

- identify the genre
- introduce the main characters
- establish the narrative
- pose the enigma which can be solved only by watching the programme
- give us transmission details.

Generally it achieves this by using key presentational devices:

- edited highlights of action and drama
- close-ups of recognisable characters/stars
- appropriate music, often the theme tune which we will learn to recognise
- a voice-over for continuity and added explanation
- graphics sequences to reinforce the programme's name.

ACTIVITY

MAKING A TRAILER

In order to complete this task you need to have access to a drama programme that you can view more than once.

Watch the programme and make notes about the genre, narrative and characters. Then, working in a small group, decide on the elements that you think should be included in a trailer. Remember that your ultimate aim is to attract an audience. You might like to use a chart like the one below to record your ideas.

	Trailer for	Trailer for
Title. What does this suggest? How have graphics been used?		
Music. How does the music fit the action: pace and style?		
Voice-over. How is this used? What information is given?		
Characters. Comment on types and stereotypes; stars		
Genre. What identifiers are there?		
Narrative. How have action codes been used? What is the enigma and how has it been posed?		

When you have agreed on the main elements, use a storyboard to design your trailer. At this point you will need to decide on the commentary: how will you combine music from the programme with dialogue and a voice-over?

Once you have completed your storyboard you could present your ideas to the rest of your class or you could include it with other work on audiences in your coursework folder. Alternatively, if you have access to editing facilities you could edit your trailer and submit it together with a written report and evaluation.

Opening sequences

Opening sequences are very important in attracting the attention of the audience.

ACTIVITY

Look at opening sequences from a variety of television dramas. For each programme answer the following questions:
- What information does the title give us?
- How do the graphics prepare us for the programme?
- How has music been used to reflect the pace and style of the programme?
- What characters are introduced to us? What expectations do we have of them?
- How have narrative codes been used?
- What conventional genre identifiers are included?

Choose two of the programmes you have analysed and write a report to present to the rest of your group.

By now you should be familiar with the codes and conventions employed by television producers in giving an identity to their programmes.

ACTIVITY

MAKING A TREATMENT

Choose a current drama programme that you are familiar with. Write a treatment for the first episode of the new series and storyboard the opening sequence. Justify any changes you have made to the presentation. Discuss your ideas with the rest of your group; select one proposal and make a group presentation to the rest of the class.

You have already learnt how the same story can be told in different ways. In order to explore the language of television drama further, carry out the following activity.

ACTIVITY

Look at the opening sequence from a story printed below:

❢ Dr Smith arrives for work to find that a patient has died during the night and a rival doctor thinks that there has been a misdiagnosis. Dr Smith's lover is having second thoughts and keeps phoning up during working hours. Nurse Jones is late for work again and the canteen is closed because of industrial action by the staff. ❢

Your task is to write a script from the treatment and to give details of sets and locations complete with camera positions. You will need to decide:
- which genre of drama your version is so that you can include identifiers for the audience
- how enigmas will be posed
- how you will establish characters
- what audio codes you will employ
- what visual codes you will use
- how you will organise the narrative into different scenes
- how you will maintain continuity.

If you have the opportunity you could storyboard and then shoot your sequence.

Television adaptations of famous books

British cinema and television have a great respect for Britain's literary heritage: the novels, plays and poetry produced by British writers. Many film and television projects start from well-known novels. In recent years the BBC's serialisations of *Pride and Prejudice* and *Middlemarch* were hugely popular. *Sense and Sensibility* has been a box office success. So clearly there is a mass audience for such adaptations.

ACTIVITY

CONTENT ANALYSIS
Use a magazine like the *Radio Times* to find out how many television dramas listed in it are based on books. Add to the list any films you can remember which are based on books, e.g. *Schindler's List*, *Jurassic Park*, *Shane*, *The Color Purple*.

Both film and television drama have many similarities to novels in that they use narrative, characters, plots, themes and settings. However, drama on television has an advantage over film when it comes to adapting a novel for the screen. Novels often have many characters and incidents and can be very long, whereas a film generally lasts only for about two hours. Screenplays, therefore, are much shorter than the original novels. They usually average only about 150 pages. By serialising a novel over many weeks, the television adaptation can operate on a similar scale to a novel. In the nineteenth century many novels were also serialised.

ACTIVITY

In pairs, discuss the following questions:
- What advantages to schedulers does a serial form bring?
- What effect does the serial form have on the structure of individual episodes?
- In what ways does a serial tell stories like a soap opera tells stories?
- In what ways is it different?

One of the main differences between the novel and screened drama is the absence of the storyteller. In the novel the storyteller may be there to comment on characters or events, or the storyteller may be using the first person (I) to tell the story so we are hearing the voice of the narrator (the person telling the story). Sometimes films use this convention but not very often. Film language has different ways of telling the story.

ACTIVITY

FILM LANGUAGE
Refresh your memory by looking back at your work on film narrative for *Beauty and the Beast* (Chapter 1). The work on the language of comics in Chapter 6 will also help.

In pairs, make a list of how a producer of television drama could:
- show things from the hero's point of view
- help establish a sense of setting: studio or location
- establish the feelings of the character if he or she was happy
- establish that the character was sad
- create atmosphere
- create audience expectation through suspense.

It is worth remembering that more people will see a production on television than will ever read the original, although many go on to read the book because of seeing the television version. One of television's key attributes is its ability to popularise texts and open them to larger audiences. In doing so television brings itself prestige by associating itself with Britain's literary

FIG 8.5 *The BBC's adaptation of the novel* Pride and Prejudice *was very popular*

past. The world market is very interested in such productions and so these can be successfully exported to other countries.

A C T I V I T Y

ADAPTING A LITERARY TEXT

Choose a book you have studied or particularly enjoy which is set in the past. Here are some pre-production tasks.

❶ Cast the main parts for a television adaptation. Be prepared to justify your choices.

❷ Research locations for your adaptation. You will need to use pictures in history and geography books or from CD-rom material. What problems would you have in being able to use the locations you choose?

❸ Make concept sketches for key characters' costumes and hairstyles.

❹ Make an oral presentation in support of your proposal to adapt this particular book in terms of audience appeal. You will need to highlight its visual potential and its similarities to past successful dramas.

❺ Take a key scene from the book. Prepare a shooting script with camera angles, location and acting suggestions, use of symbols, etc.

❻ Make suggestions for appropriate music for the title sequence.

Pre-production work is essential in television drama because such programmes are so expensive to produce. This means that often the whole reputation of an organisation can ride on the success of such a big investment.

3

EXAMINATIONS

Introduction

At present two examination boards offer GCSE Media Studies: Southern Examinations Group (SEG) which is based in England, and Welsh Joint Education Committee (WJEC) which is based in Wales. (However, it is likely that the Northern Examination Association and the Midland Examining Group will offer GCSEs in the future.) Both boards draw candidates from all parts of England, Wales and Northern Ireland. In broad terms the two syllabuses require the same kinds of knowledge, skills and understanding. They do, however, have slightly different ways of assessing your work. You should make sure that you know, with the help of your teacher, the precise requirements in assessment terms of the syllabus you are following. All the work in this book will provide experience and appropriate examples of the kind of work which is required by the different syllabuses as evidence of your achievements. Your teacher will help you to present your best work for your GCSE assessment.

9

Examining the examinations

Coursework

An exciting part of your course is the emphasis it puts on coursework; both the syllabuses ask you to present some of the best work you have done in your course for the final assessment. This gives you the opportunity to show the quality of work you can produce without the pressure of the examination room. It means you can really develop your own interests and work on long-term projects. Enthusiastic soap opera, pop music, comic or crime series buffs can build up their knowledge and competencies. Your enthusiasms can become your studies, so if work sounds a painful word, remember that in media studies work can also become a lifelong pleasure. And as you have seen, you will be faced by lots of challenging and difficult ideas as you really get down to examining the media.

Some of the work you will be set will seem familiar. You may be asked to write reports or essays which discuss media texts in detail, to keep journals of your viewing habits, or to write TV or radio scripts. This kind of work is very similar to lots of English work you have to do. Often you will be asked to present your work to the group in a variety of ways. In the WJEC syllabus you can be recorded (audio or video) doing this and this can be a coursework assignment. You can make a case for a media product, argue for a particular point of view on a contentious media issue, give a talk illustrated by audio or video clips, present your findings from a media investigation, or try to sell your advertising campaign or treatment for a media product. These are all important skills in the media industries, where you need to be able to demonstrate your abilities in these kinds of situations. In media studies you will be asked to do different kinds of writing which will be allied to pictures. For example, you may be asked to write a commentary on a series of pictures you have collected on women in advertising, or to deconstruct an advertisement by writing categories on it.

Another type of work you will be asked to do is practical work, You can bring all kinds of skills to this work as media work demands lots of different kinds of practical skills. You can use the skills you are developing in drama, music, design and technology, art and information technology (IT) to help you. Practical work such as storyboarding, designing a cover, creating a comic character, making a newspaper front cover, planning make-up and costume, and making models and gadgets should be plentiful. Media studies can reward skills in designing and drawing, performing, make-up and modelling, as well as written and oral skills.

There are also other specific media skills to develop: research skills through content analysis, focus groups, surveys and interviews of all kinds; broadcasting skills; and editing skills in print and non-print media products.

Practical work is not necessarily meant for an audience. It is a way of learning by doing. We are sure that during your course you will have some spectacular disasters; everyone does. Sometimes the columns of newspapers won't fit; you may accidentally publish a misleading or inaccurate or even illegal story; your magazine may collapse when you thought you had the perfect solution; you may have spectacular editorial disagreements. You need to learn to talk through your failures and disappointments so that you can understand what you have learnt from the experience. Practical work then is a way of thinking. Even things that have not worked out can be reflected on and used in coursework. You can write commentaries or reflect on your work through your media log. You can always gain valuable insights into media practices. These are carried out by people like you who decided to specialise in certain aspects of the media, not by robots. What we experience in the media is a result of very human decisions and sometimes even happy accidents.

Whatever the activities, it is important that the work you present as coursework is your best work. You should always be trying to use your media knowledge and skills in presenting your work. This means demonstrating that you can use media language confidently and appropriately, and that you understand the appropriate media concepts and the issues raised by them. Throughout this book you will find images of young people examining the media and very often we have used the work of past students for you to examine.

Production skills

Media studies is a subject which encourages you to develop both your practical and your production skills. Many tasks set will include a practical element: for example the storyboard, the script, the design and layout details, the mock-up, and the paste-up.

This unit has been written to give you some suggestions about how to plan and carry out your own media productions which can develop from the practical work you do. This is a very specialist area which needs support from your teachers for reasons such as accessibility of equipment, appropriateness of approach, suitability of materials, training in use of equipment, knowledge of safety procedures.

The most important point to remember is that producing the final artefact (such as the radio tape, the newspaper or the video) is the easy part provided you have completed the first stage, **the planning stage**, properly. The more time you spend planning, researching and rehearsing, the better the final production will be. Good pre-production is the key to good work!

Pre-production

You must begin by establishing the target audience for your media production. This may be straightforward because the brief you have been given may outline it. Nevertheless, further research is always a good idea. This book has introduced you to a range of ways of researching the audience: surveys, focus groups, questionnaires. You should always compile a profile of your audience. For instance, if you are producing a teenage magazine then you should find out what teenagers like to read about; alternatively if you are producing a leaflet to promote a local business then you will need to ask the managers what kind of information and what kinds of images they would like included.

You may also need to undertake some research into existing media texts, similar to the ones that you are hoping to emulate. For example, if you are planning a pop radio programme then listening to Radio 1 and your local stations would be a good idea. Content analysis is a good way to prepare.

Of course, you may decide to break with conventions and produce something that is unique; this is fine provided you know why you are changing things. In other words, to break with conventions you must first know what those conventions are! This is essential because otherwise you simply finish up drawing more attention to what you are seeking to expose.

Radio

Planning for radio work

Obviously you must begin with a script! Remember that radio is not a visual medium and adheres to its own codes and conventions. The voices and the sound effects (SFX) have to convey all the meaning to the audience. If you are scripting a radio play, you need to ensure that changes of scene or location are obvious.

Look at the radio script below. It is an extract from a short, clearly highly stereotypical drama. Read it through in your group and then decide how Scene 2, at school, will fade into Scene 3 with mother discussing the 'problem' with a neighbour.

Dialogue	Music/SFX
Scene 1	
	Introductory music (signature tune – light orchestral) 20 seconds
Father: (loudly) Don't slam the . . .	
	SFX: door slamming

(quieter) door!

Mother: You didn't have to be quite so harsh with her!	SFX: dishes being cleared; footsteps receding
Father: Was I? I didn't mean to be. It's just that if she is going to the disco tonight then I want to collect her.	SFX: tap running (in the distance)
	SFX: cup being placed in saucer
Son: Sure dad: that's fine but 10 o'clock is far too early for someone of her age!	SFX: Rustling newspaper
Father: (voice raised) Her age! She's only a child.	
Mother: (distant, as if from kitchen) She's 16 actually!	
	Fading Out
Scene 2	
	Fade in to sounds of school cloakroom: background chatter – 10 seconds, fade out
Friend: What's the matter?	SFX: locker being shut
Daughter: It's my dad, he wants to collect me at 10 tonight . . .	SFX: door closing in the distance

As practice you could record this script.

Recording your script

Ideally you should use two cassette recorders, both with pause buttons. The first is record your script; if you have an external microphone, it should be fitted to this recorder. The second will provide your sound effects and music; these need to have been pre-recorded and someone will need to fade them in and out at the appropriate times.

If you have planned well and rehearsed thoroughly you should be able to record your script in its entirety without the need to edit.

Remember to check your equipment carefully before you begin recording and try to do this in a soundproofed room.

Video

Planning for a video production

Once you have studied your brief, your first task is to produce a treatment (i.e. the broad details of the production) covering details such as what information you are trying to convey for a documentary or a synopsis of a plot for a drama; what characters will appear; what length it will be; and where it will be filmed.

When your treatment has been approved, you will then need to devise a storyboard. This is a way of showing, in sketch form, what you expect to appear in the final production. It does not matter if you are not very good at drawing, stick figures and basic outlines will be sufficient. The storyboard also needs to give instructions to the camera operator about the types of shot you want. The most common ones are:

- **The long shot (LS).** This will give the audience a broad view of the characters and location.
- **The medium shot (MS).** This shot focuses more closely on one element within the scene.
- **The close-up (CU).** This focuses very closely on an object or someone's face.

You may also want to include reference to the **zoom** when you want to move from, say, an MS to a CU; the **panning shot** when the camera moves horizontally across a location or between two characters; and the **tracking shot** when the camera moves towards or away from a scene or character. But beware of using these combi-

nations too frequently; the result will be a seasick viewer!

The third element which needs to be included in your storyboard is the sound track. Depending on the production you are planning, this may include:

- **dialogue:** the script between the characters
- **voice-over:** the voice of someone (not shown) explaining or linking scenes
- **music:** important in creating atmosphere, but select it carefully and make sure that it is appropriate for both the subject matter and your target audience
- **sound effects:** the sounds that enhance the action, e.g. a siren, an explosion, footsteps or creaking doors.

The blank storyboard shown in Figure 9.1 on page 182 can be photocopied and used to help you plan your programme.

Always research your locations carefully, ensuring you have permission to use them.

Always follow the proper safety procedures when dealing with electrical cables.

Videoing your storyboard

Check your equipment thoroughly. Make test shots in your selected locations before your shoot and check the lighting, camera positioning, decor and props. Finally, rehearse carefully and, if you have time, shoot each scene twice. Use a tripod whenever possible.

Print-based production

If you have been asked to produce a leaflet, a newspaper, a magazine or an advertising campaign, you have two choices:

- cut and paste
- computer generated.

The cut-and-paste method is as its name suggests: you cut images and words from source materials, usually magazines or newspapers, and

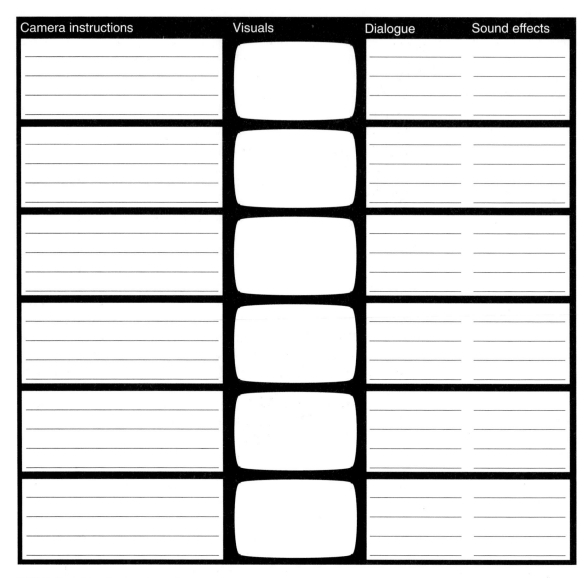

Camera instructions	Visuals	Dialogue	Sound effects

FIG 9.1 *A blank storyboard*

you paste them together according to your own planned sketches. It is a particularly effective way of producing a magazine front cover. Additional lettering can be added by using letraset.

Computer-generated texts can also be used as part of a cut-and-paste project: text can be word-processed and then pasted alongside found images.

You may have access to desk-top publishing, animation and graphics packages. These can be very useful, particularly for leaflet and advertising/packaging designs. But do take care, it is not your computer skills which are being assessed! You will still need to take conventions and institutional constraints into consideration.

Even if your artwork is not brilliant, you will learn more about production by using your own work. Some of the material you collect or download from a computer may also be in copyright or may be licensed. It is never a good idea to pretend that someone else's work is your own production. However, cut-and-paste techniques are a good way of learning about the processes of production work. This is a very complicated issue on which you will need advice from your teacher when you are preparing your work for examinations.

The main points to consider when planning a print-based production include:

Colour You may not always be able to use this, but if you can, select wisely and be sure to use the most appropriate ones. For instance, magazine front covers generally use a lot of primary colours such as red and yellow because these colours help the magazine to stand out more on the shelf. Green is less frequently used unless it is for a Christmas edition when a dark shade is often combined with red and gold.

Font size Do not be tempted to select too many different sizes. Remember, you must make a conscious decision to alter font sizes and you must be able to explain why you have done so.

Typeface Again, do not select too many different ones. Print out a short sentence in all the available types and select the most appropriate ones for your particular medium. Remember, serif fonts have a more traditional look, whilst sans serif fonts appear more modern. Think carefully about the image you want to portray and select a typeface that will reflect it.

Audience

Production work is always aimed at an audience. It is an exciting challenge and both syllabuses insist on it. So you will get the opportunity to make your own media product for an audience either on your own or more likely in a group. Whether you are publishing a magazine, making a film or running a campaign, you should have certain key questions in mind.

- What am I making?
- How will I make it?
- Who will read it?

Defining your audience, as we keep on repeating, is crucial as this will shape your product. It will help you decide what the aims of your production are. If you have these then the task will be much easier to envisage.

Evaluation

Notebooks/journals are a useful idea as a record of the process of the production. You should organise regular tutorials/report backs to the teacher so that key questions can be raised. You can use sections of this along with the final product. It can be part of the evaluation.

Evaluation can be a frightening word. It only means to measure what you have done using media language to see how successful or otherwise your production was. You can present your evaluation in both syllabuses in written form, and in the WJEC syllabus you have the option of an oral presentation.

The following headings are useful ways in which to organise your thoughts.

Pre-production

- Did you do any research before you started? For instance, if you were making a sequence in a horror film, did you examine any?
- Did you do any content analysis? What did you notice?
- Did you flick through magazines for ideas about a feature for your new magazine? Or did you examine some record covers to give you ideas for a visual style for your new product?
- Did you use survey techniques or a focus group to test your ideas on?
- Did you research what materials and technologies were available to you?
- How did these modify your approach?

Remember that you will be assessed not on the technology you use, but on the way you use the technology you have. A paper and pencil is a technology! There is some evidence of students being more impressed by the technological tricks they can perform than with the quality of the media meanings they create. As we have tried to emphasise, examining the media means exploring the ways in which the media make meanings.

- How did you focus the task? Did some things become more important than others? Did you prioritise?
- Does your work raise problems of copyright? Does it raise ethical issues?
- What kinds of other research did you do: location, archive, visits, library, listings?

Production

- What was your role (briefly)?
- What kinds of problems did you encounter? Concentrate on those which made you modify the presentation.
- Why does the product look and/or sound like it does? Does it have a style?
- What did you intend it to mean?

Post-production

- What did people think of the final version?
- Did you do any follow-up research: reader questionnaires, for instance?
- Could you sell it to an audience?
- What needs to change?

Media production work can then be fitted to your particular interests and skills. It can be fun, exhausting and frustrating. You need to be both creative and critical. You will need plenty of ideas but learn to make judgements. You should finish up as a better communicator. With the kind of technology available to you, you cannot

hope to achieve industry standard. The Disney movie *Toy Story* had thousands of storyboards and computers with huge memories. This does not mean, however, that you cannot achieve high-quality work within the constraints of your technology. Care, precision and pride are essential ingredients. Here are some useful tips:

1 Keep to deadlines. Work does not go away.
2 Get in the habit of jotting down things as you work on the different activities.
3 Be co-operative in groups, but make sure your views are considered.
4 Take control of your own learning. Interview people you know – older family members are a rich resource.
5 Be bold and inventive. Do not copy things that exist. Make them better by adding to the traditions.
6 Present your work carefully. Presentation is a key media skill.
7 Use your own interests and experience to motivate yourself. You may be a band member, a fan, a compulsive drawer or a member of a sports team: use your expertise.
8 Respond positively to questions about your work. Questions are the key to being a good media student. You should, of course, be asking them as well.

Finally, what do you think you have learnt? This should give you an opportunity to show your understanding of media language, concepts such as forms, genre, narrative, representation, audiences and media organisations. You can illustrate this point by exploring what alterations you would make if you had to produce the same piece again.

So, enjoy your studies and build on the pleasures of the media you enjoy already.

The written paper

The final written paper from both examination boards counts for 50 per cent of your final assessment. The best preparation is to work at the approaches outlined in this book, rather than needing to swot at the last minute. The reason for this is that both written papers are based on the kind of work with which you have become familiar in this book. The examination boards do this in different ways, although they are looking for the same kinds of knowledge, concepts and skills in this final part of your course. If during the course you have developed your skills in explaining and presenting your ideas and studying a wide variety of media texts, the written papers will hold no terrors for you.

SEG: controlled test This examination board specifies one study area in each year of the examination and bases the final assessment on this. It then sets a series of tasks on this area which you can research before you sit the paper. In 1997 the specified area was British soap operas.

In the controlled test you are given an idea or situation and you have to work your way through a series of tasks which are linked together. You have a period of four hours in controlled conditions to complete the different tasks. These tasks call on a range of skills that you have been developing in your media course, and you have to apply these to the new situation you are given.

WJEC: written paper This is a text-based written paper. Rather than being given a situation, you are given stimulus materials. These vary from year to year but always include some print-based texts and some audio-visual texts. Again, you have to apply your knowledge and skills to this material. The questions are linked so that you can really focus your thinking and ideas on the stimulus material. You are shown the material for 30 minutes in the room where you take the written paper, and have another two hours to complete the questions on the paper.

With both approaches to the final part of your assessment it is a good idea to work under the pressure of time. This is an essential media skill

anyway! The WJEC paper has been running since 1988, but the controlled test will be taken for the first time in 1997 so the examples in the next section are all taken from WJEC candidates' responses.

Remember, all media examiners are looking for the same kinds of things in coursework as in the controlled tests and written papers. Examiners will always reward positively:

- good media knowledge and appropriate use of media language, especially when you can give examples
- good readings of media products which show understanding of concepts such as genre, narrative, stereotyping and target audience
- good skills in presenting ideas for media products and good skills in being able to explain them.

So if you have worked hard at the coursework, you will be rewarded in the final assessment.

Improving your performance

Describing media texts

To be able to examine a media text, you need to be able to start by saying what the text is about or contains. Very often in your course you will need to explain the texts you are using as examples. You will often need to tell other people about the main features of a text.

In 1993, WJEC candidates had four trailers from different situation comedies as the stimulus material. They were asked to briefly describe one of the trailers. Examine the answers given by two of the candidates on the next page.

In terms of what these two descriptions tell us of the content/story of the trailer, there is very little to choose between them. They emphasise different bits. However, the second answer demonstrates that the candidate is aware of the construction through shots and

Answer 1

In the extract there is a man with short brown hair. He's about 30. He dresses quite old. He is taking a picture of two women in the same dress and an old bloke. He tells the old bloke that if he steps to the left, he will step in dog muck but before he finished the sentence the old bloke stepped to the left. Then the bloke taking the picture said smile and took the photo. Then it goes on to where they are all stuck in a boat on a lake. The old bloke says 'Let's go for a nice day out in the country' and we end up on the set of *Apocalypse Now*! Then it goes on and the old bloke is going from a field to an old spooky looking house.

Answer 2

The trailer begins with a close-up of the photographer who tells Mr Meldrew that if he steps to the side he will be standing in a large pile of dog mess. A voice-over says 'What could be nicer than a summer's day in the open air?' You then see a long shot of Victor, his wife and her friend stuck in a pond. Next there is a low angled shot of Victor walking up to a dark, mansion-like house, followed by a close-up shot of Victor's hand pulling the door bell. Throughout this the voice-over says 'But it's only just begun. Will Victor have more than one foot in the grave?' You see a freeze frame telling you the show is on in half an hour. Screen fades to black.

voice-over of the text, which is an important skill in media studies. This kind of awareness should be built up throughout your course in practical, production and textual analysis work.

Such knowledge will be useful when you have to do questions like these, as well as when you have to describe an extract in the examination room. Here are some typical questions and activities that might be used by WJEC and SEG.

WJEC

Describe a situation comedy, comic, special interest magazine, detective series, radio station, regional news programme, animated cartoon or star.

SEG

1 Outline the features of a major newspaper.
2 Summarise the points that make a successful film, drawing on examples of film success.
3 Give an account of the main elements that make a successful situation comedy.
4 Summarise the main elements that you would expect to find in a successful pop group.

Reading media texts

Better candidates in media studies are able to interpret the signs in the text, using its conventions to guide the reading. Here are some typical types of questions which the WJEC uses to test this skill.

1 In 1995 an extract from a *Flintstones* cartoon was used. One of the most important things about cartoons is humour, so what are the textual signs which audiences might find funny? The answers can be very varied: jokes, the situations, the animation, the setting, the characters. Most candidates can identify such elements; good candidates go on to explain the relationship to the audience through the use of typical features.
2 In 1992 the extract consisted of the title sequences of five regionally based soap operas. An important point about the television organisations which produce soap operas is that the region is used as a selling point to attract mass audiences. So questions focused on how the title sequences represented the region in which the soap opera was set. Good candidates could show how typical features of soap operas could be linked to audiences through the concepts of media representations and media organisations.
3 In 1993 a story from *The Beano* and a story from *Mandy and Judy* were used. One of the most important things about the

representation of character in comics for young people is stereotyping. So a question was set about how Dennis' behaviour was stereotypical. Better candidates could show how his comic presentation was an exaggeration; how he was simplified into a series of typical behaviours; and how these identified him as a typical character who had an audience appeal to young boys especially.

You can see how you need to be able to read the signs in media texts and relate them to the key concepts which you have been exploring in this book. Wide experience of this kind of work will help you gain more marks on the written paper. Your work should concentrate especially on key conventions of different kinds of media texts and the central issues they raise about the key concepts. The more kinds of texts you explore, the wider your knowledge will be and the better a reader of media texts you will become.

Practical work

The two boards differ in the emphasis which is given to this in the written papers: WJEC makes it count for about 25 per cent of the written paper, whilst SEG makes it count for about 60 per cent of the final paper. This is to do with the way they organise coursework. From your point of view, they both look for the same kinds of things: the ability to generate and present media ideas and proposals; skills in pre-production activity; and ability in evaluating your ideas. This book is full of such activity. Here are some of the questions and activities that have been used by WJEC in the past and some which might be appropriate for SEG.

WJEC

1 Make suggestions for a title sequence for a new soap opera to be based in your region. You may use the storyboard to help you. (1992)

2 Design a contents page for a special interest or hobby magazine. Explain the reasons for your design. (1994)

3 Make suggestions for a new cartoon character who works for the environment. Suggest a possible storyline that might be used in the cartoon series. (1995)

SEG

1 (a) Write a proposal (or brief summary) of your ideas for a new pop music, early morning show. Include ideas on format, presenter, music mix and target audience.

  (b) Plan a running order for the first show.

  (c) Outline the key points which, in your view, will make the show successful.

You can see from these examples that the kind of work you have been encouraged to do in this book supports this kind of work in the examination. The best preparation is to regularly present and discuss your ideas with other students. You can then develop your understanding of the media on the basis of practical experience and a wide range of media examples.

Both examination boards produce candidate responses to written papers and your teacher should be able to get hold of these easily for you.

Useful addresses

WJEC: 245 Western Avenue, Cardiff CF5 2YX.

SEG: Publications Department, Stag Hill House, Guildford, Surrey GU2 5XJ.

Glossary

Most of the important words and the concepts they represent are explained in the text as they occur. This glossary provides a reference section for the revision of key terms.

Access The media are influential in our society and so it is of great importance to be able to have access to such powerful ways of communicating with mass audiences. One of the key issues here is who controls the media and therefore who decides what kinds of representations are made. Organised pressure groups can create opportunities for their messages and views to be presented in the media. Another important use of the word is when media organisations claim that they are creating greater access to their products through better technology and cheaper prices. It is often connected to the issue of freedom of choice.

Alternative media texts These are texts which aim to be deliberately different to mainstream texts. They often do this by making fun of traditional texts (by parody, for example), by offering extreme or unusual viewpoints, or by promoting the viewpoints of under-represented groups.

Alternative working practices The growth of technology, especially print-based technology but also camcorder technology, has allowed people to make their own media texts. They have often developed different ways of working. The values in this are enjoyment and commitment rather than profit; they are small scale for well-defined audiences, and individuals tend to be responsible for many more aspects of production. They often have localised distribution networks.

Anchorage Originally this meant the part that captions played in closing down the meaning of photographic images. By extension, it can also mean the role of a media presenter in anchoring the presentation of different kinds of media presentations: the newscaster, the sports presenter and the game show host, for example.

Audience The audience is central to the interactive process of media communication. There is an enormous range of important issues connected with the study of audiences. At GCSE level the following interconnected aspects are important.

Audience engagement This is the way that audiences relate to a media text and interact with it to create meanings. You may not interpret a text in the same way as someone else. The debate over teenage magazines is a good example of this.

Audience expectations These are the kinds of things which audiences expect from the texts. Much media output is organised in typical ways in terms of things like narrative and genre. Predictability is important. However, media producers are always looking to create variations in the patterns. These differences, which are often quite small, help to brand particular organisations or texts. So you are able to recognise that *News At Ten* is both like and unlike *The Nine O'Clock News*, or that a soap opera is like and unlike a television serial. Sometimes media producers set out to shock or surprise the audience by breaking with audience expectations.

Audience foreknowledge This is what an audience brings to a media product, such as knowledge about a star or knowledge of the book on which a television programme was based.

Audience identification This is the way in which audiences feel they are related to aspects of media production. They prefer one newspaper to another one because it feels more like them. They like particular characters in programmes or particular types of programmes. This raises many complex issues: stalking, imitation, role models, fans and obsessions, for example.

Audience placement Media producers try to find out what their audiences want and meet those needs by using a range of strategies. In this book we have tried to place you by putting in lots of photographs of students working on and in the media, by using examples of students' work, and by addressing you directly. We hope that it has worked and that you feel able to identify with the book.

Audience research All media organisations research their audiences. In this book we have tried to introduce you to some of the ways in which you can do this. The target audience of a media production is essential in your own production work.

Bias This is a difficult word for the media student, but a word which is used all the time in media debates. It is important for you, as a media student, to grasp that all media texts are constructed in different ways for different purposes. Some of these seek to influence and persuade, some to entertain and give pleasure. Discussions about bias tend to concern the first category. Does the text give a fair, balanced view of an issue, argument or way of life? The answer to this question will very much depend on our original viewpoint and the way we interact with the text.

Connotation This describes the process of interpretation in which individual signs have a range of meanings. The linguistic sign red can, for example, have a range of meanings – stop, warning, love, blood.

Control Some media controls are obvious, such as legal controls like film and video classifications. There can also be ethical controls, for example on the use of stories or photographs of famous people. Some controls can be less obvious, such as the ways in which the major film organisations try to control the means of distribution. It is a complex area of study.

Convention This is the usual way in which the media present something. For example, the news is read sitting down, whilst the weather is presented from a standing position. Conventions are important in linking the texts to the audiences.

Cropping This is a technique by which a photograph is cut to a required shape for newspapers and magazines. It is important because in the cropping process certain things are given priority and other parts are discarded.

Decoding This is the process of reading the codes of media texts to interpret them. This book introduces the concept of media language as a way of decoding media texts.

Deconstruction We use this process all the time in the book to break media organisations and texts into individual parts to explore the conventional ways in which they seek to make meaning.

Editing This is the last stage in the production of print or film where parts of the project are pieced together. One set of meanings is created in the process of selection/omission and ordering/ sequencing of material. It is a crucial skill for media students to have and they should gain experience of it in a range of practical tasks.

Enigma This refers to the way different kinds of texts set narrative puzzles or teasers for the audience which are resolved in the text. Examples are numerous: front pages, opening sequences, posters, trailers. It is part of the pleasure of the text that these enigmas become clear to the audience as the plot unfolds. Sometimes everything is resolved, as in a crime mystery, and the narrative is closed. Sometimes the ending itself is enigmatic, leaving the possibility of another production or a doubt in the mind of the audience. It applies to non-fiction narratives as well.

Fan Fans are often stereotyped as immature, young and obsessional. Yet they are important as they often have detailed media histories available to them, unavailable to the general audience. Some fans become media producers themselves: commentators on sport, animators, special effects people.

Fanzine A fanzine is a small circulation publication usually produced and sold independently to a closely defined audience. Technology has improved the quality of the presentation of these magazines and anyone can now, with energy and commitment, produce his or her own.

Genre This is a type of film or programme; a category which defines a text by its similarities to others. In order to recognise genre, we usually look for repeated narrative forms, characters, settings and iconography. Genre is an important area to study as it explores the relationships between texts and audiences.

Icon An icon is a sign which looks like the thing itself and is therefore easy to read. For example, a photograph of Ryan Giggs is iconic. A good exercise is to try to make up a human face in as many different ways as you can using a variety of objects. You will see when the attempts stop looking like human faces. It remains iconic as long as it looks like the thing itself. This is very important in the language of comics and in the computer environment where you click on to icons.

Iconography Iconography is a collection of easily recognised signs. So title sequences have repeated signs which identify the programme genre as a regionally based soap, national news or American cop show. The iconography of a western film could include a gun, Stetson, saloon and horse, for example.

Juxtaposition This is the process of putting different kinds of media materials side by side to create meaning. For instance, a Liverpudlian accent may connote pop music but when placed next to a standard English accent in a sit-com may connote class-based humour. In soap operas stories may run alongside each other. Although these might share some of the same characters, some characters will not know what is happening in other storylines; the audience is given meaning which the characters are not. A news organisation may juxtapose a sad story with a happy story to keep the audience's attention or to appeal to different members of the audience.

Market This is the whole potential audience for a media production: anyone who might buy, watch or hear it. Media products are packaged and branded for particular markets.

Mediation This is the way in which messages are channelled through the different media. Each medium has its own way of doing this, so different media can present the same material in different ways using their own language.

Metonym This is a sign which stands for more than itself. When we say that all the hands in the factory are on strike, we are making the hands stand for the workers. So the ticking of a clock in a film or radio production can represent time passing slowly or tension; a flag with a dragon on it can represent Wales; a theme tune represents a programme; Big Ben chiming can represent the news on radio.

Plugs/plugging/plugger Plugs are deliberate attempts to create advance publicity. Plugging is therefore an important media activity and takes many forms: on the front pages, in chat shows, in magazine interviews, in record plays on radio. The plugger is employed to find ways of promoting the new product, preferably without paying for it.

Point-of-view shot (POV) When this is used in a film, television drama or comic, we see events from the point of view of the character, thus linking the audience and character more closely.

Reconstruction This is a technique used in documentaries that employs actors to present past events.

Role model This is a figure from the media who influences the audience. Sometimes such figures are imaginary, like Batman who fights to clear the streets of Gotham City of all kinds of anti-social behaviour. It is not only a media phenomenon, as in real life we often have people on whom we model ourselves. It is, of course, very controversial because if we choose the wrong role models we can be adversely affected. This is a complicated issue which you will have begun to explore in your work on media effects.

Semiology This is the study of signs.

Set-up This is a scene, often in a documentary, which appears to be unfolding naturally as we watch but which has been pre-planned or even rehearsed beforehand.

Star A star has a manufactured image which has a complex relationship with the real person. A star image is a marketing device which depends on the empathy and involvement of the audience.

Storyboard This is a visual plan of what is to be filmed. It is presented in squares, indicating shots, actions and sound. It provides an essential means of visualising the final version. Expertly done, it is remarkable how like the finished version storyboards are. Excellent examples are available for *Star Wars* and *The Raiders of the Lost Ark*. Many activities in media studies require skills in visualising the finished product. It is always worth improving your drawing skills.

Talking head This term is used for an expert speaker who appears in news or documentary as a head and shoulders, giving opinions, information, expert comment. Some television dramatists (Bleasdale, Bennett) have borrowed the technique to give authenticity and attention to a character.

Technology This term covers equipment of any sort used in the making of media texts.

Transcript This is a written version of speech.

Viewpoint Some media productions have explicit viewpoints: buy this product; vote for this party; listen to this case. Others have implicit viewpoints which can be read by deconstructing the text and looking for the gaps and omissions. Most have both. Sometimes it is very difficult to see implicit viewpoints because we share the viewpoint of the media producer.

Voice-over This is a technique in which a voice speaks over the pictures in a film or programme. In documentary they can be narrators who know everything or who provide linking commentary on what has happened. Often in a narrative film the speaker shapes the narrative. It is a central feature of animation and many famous voices have never been seen. It is also an important continuity device to maintain the audience's interest between programmes.

Index